HANDBOOK ON SUSTAINABLE INVESTMENTS

Background Information and Practical Examples for Institutional Asset Owners

Swiss Sustainable Finance

CFA Institute Research Foundation

CFA Society Switzerland

Swiss Sustainable Finance

Statement of Purpose

The CFA Institute Research Foundation is a not-for-profit organization established to promote the development and dissemination of relevant research for investment practitioners worldwide.

Contents

CE Qualified Activity   CFA Institute   This publication qualifies for 4 CE credits, 0.5 SER, under the guidelines of the CFA Institute Continuing Education Program.

Foreword

Going Long

The craft and science of investing is essentially about optimising performance by either achieving the maximum future return for any given risk level or minimising risk for a defined return goal, all the while being exposed to fundamental uncertainty about the future. There is little room for additional goals in this equation.

Or so you think!

A fast-growing share of investors have recently widened their scope of analysis to criteria regarded as extra-financial. They are driven by different motivations. Adoption of sustainable investment strategies can be driven, on the one hand, by the sole motivation to hedge portfolios against knowable risks by expanding the conceptual framework to incorporate the latest best practice in risk management. Other investors focus on a long-term view and make an active bet on societal change. Recent empirical research has shown that considering sustainability factors within investment practices does not come at a cost (i.e., through a reduced opportunity set) but allows for competitive returns. Furthermore, the growing market and resulting competition in the wake of sustainable investing going mainstream has the welcome effect of compressing fees for such products. Hence, staying informed about recent trends in sustainable investing is imperative no matter what the main motivation is.

This is where this publication, prepared by Swiss Sustainable Finance (SSF) and translated by the CFA Institute Research Foundation, comes in. Its practical insights into different approaches of sustainable investments, complemented with case studies from different asset owners, permits the reader to gain a comprehensive overview of contemporary best practice in sustainable investing.

The financial industry has a long history of imposing its values and practices onto the real economy. While in the case of the increasing financialisation of our world this might have raised concerns, for sustainable investing it can turn into an opportunity. If taking on a longer-term view and rewarding corporate sustainability turns into the new normal, this might counteract the ever shorter time horizons of market participants. Such a shift is in perfect conformity with the CFA Institute mission "to lead the investment profession globally by promoting the highest standards of ethics, education, and professional excellence for the ultimate benefit of society."

Sabine Döbeli
CEO, Swiss Sustainable Finance

Christian Dreyer, CFA
CEO, CFA Society Switzerland

1. Summary of the Sustainable Investment Handbook

Part 1: Sustainable Investments in Context

Chapter 3. Sustainable Investments and Institutional Investors in Switzerland—Overview of Current Status and Developments

- Sustainable investments are increasingly important for Swiss institutional investors.

- Some cantonal pension funds have regulations that require sustainability criteria to be taken into consideration when investing.

- The Swiss market for sustainable investments is growing faster than the overall market. This includes internally managed sustainable assets of institutional investors.

Chapter 4. The Performance of Sustainable Investments—An Overview of Academic Studies

- Financial markets fail to take full account of the risks and benefits associated with a company's ESG performance. This creates potential opportunities for investors.

- This finding has been confirmed by numerous scientific studies that analyse the impact of various ESG aspects on a company's performance.

- For sustainability funds, the results are mixed. However, many studies show that sustainable investments do not adversely affect financial performance.

Chapter 5. Development of the Regulatory and Legislative Environment for Sustainable Investment

- France, the Netherlands, and the United Kingdom have the most highly developed regulation concerning sustainable investment compared with the rest of Europe.

- Swiss pension funds have a legal obligation as equity shareholders to actively vote.

- The integration of sustainability themes in the investment process is consistent with the fiduciary duties of institutional investors, if not a requirement.

Part 2: Different Approaches to Sustainable Investment and Specific Asset Classes

Chapter 6. Introduction to Different Approaches to Sustainable Investment

Chapter 7. Exclusions

- Exclusion criteria are an established approach to sustainable investment, intended to reflect the investors' values within their investments.

- Any detrimental impact on performance can be compensated by modifying the exclusion criteria, optimising the portfolio, or combining the approach with other ESG strategies.

Case Study: Velux Foundation

- A foundation increases its impact through sustainable investment.

Chapter 8. Best-in-Class Approach

- The best-in-class approach is a method for selecting businesses with a convincing record of implementing ESG measures.

- It allows the construction of diversified securities portfolios that are financially attractive and at the same time support sustainable long-term growth.

Case Study: Eltaver AG

- A family office invests in line with family values.

Chapter 9. ESG Integration Approach

- ESG integration is the explicit inclusion of ESG opportunities and risks in traditional financial analysis and investment decisions of asset managers.

- Sustainability factors can be an indicator of a company's competitive advantage and influence the longer-term assumptions of financial analysts.

- An ESG integration process takes into account the long-term growth prospects, not only making a portfolio attractive from a sustainability perspective but also improving the risk–return profile.

Chapter 9.1. Enhancing the Investment Process through ESG Integration

- An example illustrates how an ESG assessment is integrated as a key component of the investment process.
- The ESG assessment carried out by financial analysts helps them better understand the value drivers and risks of a company and creates added value for investors.

Chapter 9.2. Optimised Geographical Asset Allocation Thanks to ESG Integration

- Political, macroeconomic, and resource-oriented criteria are relevant for an optimised geographical asset allocation.
- Long-term ESG trends, which can be measured quantitatively, give an early indication of structural changes that are not analysed by mainstream investors and rating agencies.

Chapter 9.3. The Role of ESG Integration in Emerging Market Investments

- The limited availability of ESG information is one of the main challenges for an ESG integration approach in the context of emerging markets.
- Dialogue at the board level can provide access to senior management, thereby making it easier to access information.
- The ESG integration approach adds value to the investment process.

Case Study: Zurich Insurance Group

- An insurance company integrates sustainability criteria throughout its investment processes.

Chapter 10. Exercising Voting Rights

- Exercising voting rights is an important means for shareholders to express their views on what constitutes good business management.

- Detailed analysis of all agenda items requires substantial resources, which is why many investors delegate their decisions to proxy advisors.

- Although the board's proposals are seldom rejected in Switzerland, even a small percentage of "no" votes makes the company management more amenable to discussing the concerns of critical shareholders and perhaps adapting the strategy.

Case Study: Pension Fund of the City of Zurich

- A public pension fund gets involved as an active shareholder, in foreign companies too.

Chapter 11. Shareholder Engagement—Dialogue with Companies

- Shareholder engagement is a long-term process aimed at systematically promoting key ESG aspects in the business practices of portfolio companies.

- Portfolio managers can use shareholder engagement as the basis for optimised investment decisions.

- Since it is a resource-intensive and specialised process, it may make sense to delegate engagement to an independent provider or cooperate with other investors.

Case Study: PUBLICA Federal Pension Fund

- The Pension Fund of the Swiss Confederation joins forces with other public sector investors for engagement and exclusion.

Chapter 11.1. Shareholder Engagement: Experiences of a Swiss Investor Collective

- Pooling investors makes it possible to conduct an effective dialogue with companies on sustainability issues.

- If this improves company performance, all the involved investors will benefit.

Case Study: CAP Prévoyance

- A public sector pension fund focuses its investments on long-term, sustainable development.

Chapter 12. Sustainable Thematic Investments

- Sustainable thematic investments can create value as part of a stock allocation process thanks to an attractive risk/return profile.

- They can help diversify a stock allocation, since they exhibit only minor overlaps with the popular global equity indices.

- Combining sustainable thematic investments with ESG integration and active shareholder ownership principles creates an advantageous sustainability profile.

Chapter 13. Impact Investing

- Impact investments distinguish themselves from other forms of sustainable investing mainly by their intentionality to achieve a positive social or environmental impact and their commitment to report on the impact or outcome of the investments (measurability).

- The majority of impact investing funds target the delivery of at least market-rate returns and are a suitable investment vehicle to diversify investment, as returns are often uncorrelated with those of the mainstream market.

Chapter 13.1. Investments for Development

- After years of steady growth, investments for development worldwide now exceed USD30 billion. Switzerland has assumed a leading role in this area.

- This growth reflects not only a societal trend toward more sustainability but also new investment opportunities in frontier markets.

- While microfinance investments were previously the mainstay, other sectors—particularly the energy sector—are now also gaining importance.

Chapter 13.2. Microfinance

- Switzerland provides management and consulting services for 38% of global microfinance investment, making it the world market leader in this segment.

- A global microfinance index showed constant positive returns of 3–6% (in US dollar terms) in the past eleven years, thus proving that microfinance investment vehicles are extremely robust in the face of global economic weaknesses.

Chapter 14. Green Bonds

- Green bonds are a suitable instrument for funding renewable energies and hence the energy transition.

- The market for green bonds is based on voluntary standards and is gradually becoming more structured.

Chapter 15. Sustainable Infrastructure Investments

- The consideration of ESG criteria is especially appropriate in the case of infrastructure projects due to their inherent longevity and capital intensity.

- Applying ESG criteria creates added value, brings additional benefits for the environment, society, and the economy, and has the potential to make infrastructure investments more attractive.

Chapter 16. Sustainable Private Equity Investments

- Private equity investors have inherent corporate governance advantages unlike investors in other asset classes. This opens opportunities for better sustainable investments and higher investment returns.

- Compared with primary or secondary investments, direct private equity exposures offer better opportunities to integrate ESG criteria and create social benefits.

Chapter 17. Sustainable Real Estate

- Sustainable real estate today accounts for a significant share of the property market as a whole and offers great investment potential.

- Sustainable properties are economically attractive and offer risk diversification.

- Green labels, performance indicators, and benchmarking initiatives increase transparency.

Chapter 18. Integrating Sustainability into Commodity Investing

- One of the main discussions concerning commodity investments and sustainability issues revolves around the impact of physical and derivative investors on commodity prices.

- Investors in commodity derivatives fulfil an important role in food security through their contribution to lower price volatility, given that the investments are managed actively and exclude futures contracts with measurable destabilising price effects.

- ESG issues of physical commodity investments are related to price impact as well as social and environmental issues along the value chain (traceability).

Part 3: Special Themes

Chapter 19. Climate Change and Associated Risks for Investors

- Climate change regulation and its impact present growing risks for investments.
- A wide range of instruments and strategies are available to investors to help them understand, measure, and mitigate these risks.

Case Study: Nest Collective Foundation

- A pioneer in sustainable investment places greater emphasis on the carbon intensity of its portfolios.

Chapter 20. The Role of Indices in Sustainable Investment

- Virtually all the major index providers today offer numerous sustainability indices based on different sustainable investment approaches.
- On the one hand, these indices can be used as an investment universe for active investment strategies. On the other hand, they are also suitable for passive strategies implemented via index-linked funds.

Case Study: Swissport Company Pension Fund

- A tailor-made passive investment product is developed for a company pension fund.

Chapter 21. Transparency of Sustainable Investments

- Creating transparency requires effort but fosters credibility and legitimacy through lower reputational risks.
- There is no defined, generally valid standard for reporting on sustainable investments. However, this offers flexibility to develop customised solutions based on individual requirements.

Part 4: Steps to Implementation

Chapter 22. Implementing a Sustainable Investment Policy—A Practical Guide

- There is no single recipe for implementing a sustainable investment policy but rather various approaches with different objectives and impacts.

- A suitable approach can be identified for each asset class depending on the primary motivation.

- Implementation of the sustainable investment policy can be carried out internally or outsourced to external providers.

- In either case, the results should be monitored on a regular basis. Reporting on the sustainable investment policy offers transparency to different stakeholders.

2. Introduction

Over the course of more than 20 years, the advancement of sustainable investments[1] has created a large and diverse offering that includes products and services for virtually every asset class, geographical region, and investment strategy. These investments have proven themselves to be comparable with conventional investment products in terms of risk and return, in many cases providing more-effective portfolio diversification. At the same time, they make an active contribution towards bringing the economy onto a more sustainable path.

There are several reasons why institutional investors consider sustainability aspects when making investments. The three main criteria are

- complying with generally recognised international and national standards/norms or specific values defined by their own organisation within their investment activity,

- improving the risk/return profile of investments, and

- promoting sustainable development and business practices.

More and more investors who manage wealth for third parties on a fiduciary basis have added sustainability criteria to their investment policy for one or more of these reasons.[2]

Recently, new regulations governing sustainability have been introduced in many European countries. The Ordinance against Excessive Compensation in Listed Corporations (VegüV)[3] was Switzerland's first bid to make active exercising of shareholder votes on specific themes obligatory for pension funds. Pressure from various stakeholders is steadily mounting. These include NGOs, who stress the responsibility of institutional investors, and members of pension funds, who want to see their assets invested in a responsible manner.

In Switzerland, self-regulation is very important in many areas, including sustainable investment. The need to define a sustainable investment policy in a self-determined manner—as well as being as flexible as possible in its implementation—has already encouraged a number of Swiss institutional investors to go down this route. Many others have only just started discussions at top level to see whether, and how, such a step could be taken.

One thing is clear: Switzerland has already built up enormous expertise in the area of sustainable investments, and anyone embarking on that course will not be alone. The huge choice currently available might actually intimidate investors trying to get to grips with this topic for the first time. After all, it is not that simple to get a clear idea of the different approaches and decide which is most suited for a particular organisation.

Swiss Sustainable Finance (SSF) has received a number of requests over time to clarify terms or provide a clearer overview of sustainable investments both from SSF members and from other institutional investors. This Handbook is designed to meet that demand and offer a broad, readily understandable overview of sustainable investment as practised today in Switzerland and elsewhere.

The Handbook's main target audience is representatives of such institutional investors as pension funds, insurance companies, foundations, and family offices that are looking to initiate a discussion about the implementation of a sustainable investment policy or have been instructed to develop such a policy. This publication is thus aimed not only at the foundation board of trustees but also at the heads of institutional investment companies, investment specialists in general, and people who deal with investment strategies as part of their supervisory role but are not actively involved in this area on a daily basis.

The Handbook is organised into four parts:

Part 1: Sustainable Investments in Context describes the developments on this theme among institutional investors in Switzerland. One chapter examines the important question of the potential effect on the performance of an investment portfolio of applying sustainability criteria. The last chapter describes the regulatory situation in major European countries (including Switzerland).

Part 2: Different Approaches to Sustainable Investment and Specific Asset Classes is the main body of the Handbook. In this section, all the current approaches to sustainable investment are introduced and explained. In addition, specific sustainable asset classes that are becoming increasingly important are outlined.

Part 3: Special Themes explores interdisciplinary topics that are highly relevant for all sustainable investments. This includes the question of how climate change—and the measures taken to combat it—affects investment portfolios and how these impacts can be rendered measurable. Another chapter examines the role that indices play for sustainable investment. Finally, the importance of transparent reporting for sustainable investment strategies is discussed.

Part 4: Steps to Implementation is perhaps the most important part of the Handbook. In the manner of a cookbook, this lists the ingredients for defining and implementing a sustainable investment policy. All the key steps are described—from determining the main motivation to defining the investment policy and implementing the strategy—and allocated to the various actors within an organisation.

Throughout the Handbook, there are also a number of **case studies** providing insights into how sustainable investment strategies are implemented by various institutional investors. The examples include a number of pension funds (as well as one insurance company, a foundation, and a family office) and offer a varied picture of different approaches to implementing a sustainable investment policy.

Like every specialist field, sustainable investment has developed its own terminology, which often contains abbreviations (just to make things even more complicated). A short **glossary** at the end of the Handbook explains the most important terms. A more detailed version can be found on the SSF website, where it is updated regularly.[4]

Taken as a whole, the Handbook clearly shows that sustainable investments have evolved into a mature market. The general idea is for the current publication to serve as a reference work where readers can pick out the chapters most relevant to them. The first chapter in Part 2, "Introduction to Different Approaches to Sustainable Investment," highlights which approaches are applicable to which asset classes and may come in useful when deciding which chapters to prioritise. SSF hopes you enjoy reading the Handbook and discovering the strategy that best suits your own organisation.

Endnotes

[1] See the Glossary for a definition of the term "sustainable investments."

[2] See chapter 22 for background information on determining the main motivations.

[3] Swiss Federal Council. (2014). *Verordnung gegen übermässige Vergütungen bei börsenkotierten Aktiengesellschaften.* https://www.admin.ch/opc/de/classified-compilation/20132519/index.html.

[4] Swiss Sustainable Finance. (2016). *Glossary.* http://www.sustainablefinance.ch/en/glossary-_content---1--3077.html.

Part 1: Sustainable Investments in Context

3. Sustainable Investments and Institutional Investors in Switzerland— Overview of Current Status and Developments

Jean Laville
Deputy CEO, Swiss Sustainable Finance

Sustainable or responsible investments are currently gaining prominence among Swiss public pension schemes and charitable foundations.[1] 2015 was a particularly important year for pension schemes with the creation of the new Swiss Association for Responsible Investments (SVVK-ASIR), with such founding members as public pension funds Compenswiss, PUBLICA, and the Pension Fund of the Post Office. Furthermore, the association of Swiss grant-making foundations (SwissFoundations) drew up a governance code, encouraging members to include sustainability issues in their wealth management activities.

Ever-Increasing Formalisation

These new initiatives come in the wake of legislative changes by the cantons of Geneva (2014) and Vaud (2015), which now oblige their respective pension funds to comply with sustainable development and responsible investment objectives. These legislative measures compel pension funds to formalise these policy decisions in investment regulations and responsible investment charters. The same is true for foundations, where such responsible investment policies help them to formalise their values and objectives and apply them to their asset management while matching them to their risk/return profile.

A Fresh Look at Performance

The recent developments have come about following a shift in how industry participants view the impact of responsible investing on financial performance. More and more studies—both academic and practical—are showing that an investment strategy encompassing environmental, social, and governance (ESG) criteria can achieve performance in line with that of traditional investments.[2] This clarification of financial perspectives of sustainable strategies facilitates the debate within the bodies responsible for defining investment strategies. In the case of active asset management, however, choosing titles needs to be made extremely professionally; the inclusion of ESG criteria alone does not guarantee performance that keeps up with market expectations. Generally, there has been a considerable increase in the product offerings of ESG-related strategies, which, in turn, gives investors more-diversified choices and higher quality investments.

Progressing towards Greater Fiduciary Duty

Academics and finance professionals are becoming progressively more cognisant of the materiality of ESG criteria for the short-, medium-, and long-term performance of companies. Accordingly, the integration of ESG factors is increasingly considered integral to pension funds' fiduciary duty, with a view to providing members with satisfactory annuities.

The debate launched by the Freshfields report in 2005, and confirmed in the 2015 follow-up report,[3] has clearly prompted the incorporation of ESG factors in the investment process. For many players, this debate is now closed. Today, it is commonly accepted that considering ESG criteria within an investment strategy is simply part of one's natural fiduciary duty, as long as these criteria are shown to have a long-term effect on the financial performance of companies. This has even become mandatory in certain countries, with France, for example, making it compulsory for certain categories of asset holders to explain how ESG factors are included in their investment strategy.

A Wide Range of Sustainability-Related Approaches

Although sustainable investing traditionally began with corporate shares, it has since spread to many other asset classes, including corporate and government bonds, real estate, and private equity. Similarly, the early 2000s saw the emergence of thematic approaches in the environmental domain, with the inception of water-, renewable energy-, forestry-, and agriculture-related investment funds. These show mixed performances, but over the long term, a water-related investment scheme, for example, generated higher risk-adjusted returns than the global index. In the social sphere, the appearance of microfinance investment funds operating in emerging or developing countries has spurred interest among pension funds due to their stable returns and positive social impact. One-third of these investments are currently managed out of Switzerland.[4] More recently, investments for development, which seek to directly generate a positive social and environmental impact in addition to financial return, are starting to capture the attention of long-term investors managing investments in asset classes with lower liquidity (private equity).

It has also become vital for investors committed to a sustainable investment approach to keep their eye on ESG factors when exercising voting rights. Alone or in a pool, institutional investors are engaging more and more in shareholder dialogue initiatives to help influence major portfolio companies with respect to ESG issues. The dialogue favours an improved long-term performance of their investments and the adoption of better corporate sustainability practices.

The Minder Initiative has had a profound impact on the conduct of Swiss pension funds in light of the constitutional obligation to exercise voting rights related to excessive compensation practices. For pension funds that were already *en route* for a sustainable investment approach, however, the law has simply substantiated their established practices.

A Growth Market

Although the level of sustainable investment by Swiss pension funds has remained relatively low in recent years, interest is growing among major international pension funds. The success of the Principles for Responsible Investment demonstrates a move by institutional players worldwide to engage on three fronts, namely by (i) incorporating ESG issues in their investments, (ii) actively exercising their voting rights, and (iii) supporting shareholder dialogue initiatives.

The recent formalisation of sustainable investment policies by major Swiss institutions shows that attitudes are changing towards taking account of sustainability. The sector is being put under more pressure by the media, with the Swiss National Bank (SNB) coverage being a case in point.[5] This reflects an appreciation of the positive effects of sustainable finance and promotes its acceptance by the public at large.

The 2017 survey by SSF and FNG shows a constant rise in the amounts invested in various ESG-integrating strategies on the Swiss sustainable finance market. Total sustainable assets managed by Swiss asset managers has risen 18% to CHF161.8 billion. The study also illustrates that the large Swiss pension funds internally manage sustainable investments of CHF104.5 billion (with a growth of 89%), proving once again the popular support for this type of investment in Switzerland.

Endnotes

[1]Zaki, M., & Guertchakoff, S. (2016). *L'investissement durable séduit les caisses de pension (The attraction of sustainable development for pension funds)*. Bilan (26 July 2016). Available at: http://www.bilan.ch/argent-finances-plus-de-redaction/linvestissement-durable-a-plus-damis?utm_content=buffer5375d&utm_medium=social&utm_source=twitter.com&utm_campaign=buffer.

[2]Swiss Sustainable Finance. (2016). *Performance of sustainable investments. Evidence and case studies*. Available at: http://www.sustainablefinance.ch/upload/cms/user/2016_06_30_sustainableInvestment_Performance.pdf.

[3]PRI, generation foundation, & UNEP FI. (2015). *Fiduciary duty in the 21st century*. Available at: http://www.fiduciaryduty21.org/index.html.

[4]Symbiotics. (2015). *2015 Microfinance investment vehicles survey*. Market Data & Peer Group Analysis. Available at: http://www.microfinancegateway.org/library/2015-microfinance-investment-vehicles-survey-market-data-peer-group-analysis.

[5]The SNB was repeatedly criticised in the media for investments considered as controversial—a discussion which stirred public dialogue on investors' responsibility.

4. The Performance of Sustainable Investments—An Overview of Academic Studies

Alexander Zanker, CFA
Senior ESG/Quant. Strategist, LGT Capital Partners

Why ESG Factors Matter

Questioning whether integrating ESG factors into investing impacts investment performance has been the focus of both the academic world and of asset owners and investors ever since sustainable investing (SI) evolved from an ethical niche into a widely adopted investment practice. In the academic world, the majority of studies consider equity investments, due to the availability of data, and deal mainly with the influence of ESG factors on one of these three measures:

- Economic performance of companies

- Companies' cost of capital

- Performance of companies' traded shares

This article focuses on performance in terms of financial returns of individual securities and portfolios, arguing why incorporating ESG factors could influence returns and showing a presentation of empirical findings on this topic.

One of the pillars of classical finance is the concept that returns on financial assets should be driven only by their exposure to non-diversifiable economic risk (e.g., aggregate consumption). Today, other factors are also considered, as in the famous Fama–French three-factor model (which incorporates book-to-price and company size) or other extensions. The common idea here is that expected returns are driven by exposures to the various factors, and the models built on these factors enable investors to form a portfolio that delivers the highest level of diversification for a given level of expected return.

With this in mind, the exclusion of certain segments of assets due to ESG considerations, or the use of information other than the respective factors to formulate return expectations, would lead to a suboptimal portfolio that takes higher risks than necessary for a given level of expected return.

This argument is not easily discarded. So, what are the possible reasons why including ESG factors in return expectations could still be beneficial?

The "G": Governance

Providers of capital usually face the drawback that there are agents (i.e., management for companies and governments for sovereign bonds) acting on their behalf when putting their investments to work. The concept of good governance now means ensuring that these agents act in the best interest of investors, rather than their own. If financial markets fail to price agency costs implied by different levels of governance, a focus on strong governance could lead to superior return expectations. There is empirical evidence that this is indeed the case.[1,2]

The "E" and "S": Environmental and Social Aspects

Simple logic would imply that implementing high environmental and social standards leads to higher costs, which hurts a company's profitability. Also, the social welfare theorem suggests that focusing on profit maximisation on the company level should maximise overall social benefit as well. This would be the case if no externalities existed. If costs incurred for environmental or social damage are overlooked or insufficiently priced and borne by the origi-nators, companies run the risk of having to internalise higher costs resulting from new regulation or legal action. Another problem is litigation risk in rela-tion to environmental or social damage. Once again, if markets fail to price these risks correctly, taking environmental and social aspects into account when assessing return expectations could lead to superior results.

Dealing specifically with environmental topics, there are also several studies that find a positive correlation between environmental performance or events and subsequent stock performance.[3,4] It should be emphasised that as the effects of global warming unfold, triggering related governmental actions, we will be entering "uncharted territory," as there is no issue comparable to this, both in impact and scope, within the observation periods covered by the studies mentioned.

Social factors can also be related to company performance, as good social behaviour enhances a company's reputation with customers and employees and contributes to employee satisfaction. Having a more satisfied workforce ultimately reduces costs as these companies normally have lower staff turn-over, fewer incidents of fraud, and increased productivity. If markets fail to correctly assess the impact of these effects, good social performance could again lead to superior return expectations. Several papers that assess the impact of employee satisfaction on subsequent stock performance show evidence of a positive relationship between the variables.[5,6]

Overall Empirical Evidence

The previous section already presented some empirical evidence of the positive relationship between companies' performance or actions on specific ESG issues and subsequent stock returns. Another research area is the relationship between aggregate ESG measures and stock prices. In addition to studies focusing on the company level, the performance of portfolios or funds that incorporate an ESG focus in their investment policy can also be compared against broader peer groups. A third, somewhat limited source of easily accessible performance reference is ESG indices, which can be compared to regular benchmarks. With respect to overall ESG ratings, one challenge is to identify meaningful aggregate criteria used to define ESG performance in the specific context. Two studies that are very well thought out in this respect are worth mentioning. The first paper[7] tries to focus on material ESG topics only when compiling aggregate ESG indicators for single stocks. It makes use of the Sustainability Accounting Standards Board's (SASB) determination of material criteria for the different industries. Strong evidence is found that the stocks of companies that show a good performance on material ESG issues outperform weak ESG performers.

Do "Sin" Stocks Outperform?

When drawing any conclusions from studies, particularly on the individual stock level, the design of the study has to be critically assessed to establish whether it is really able to examine the relationship in question without being driven by other overlooked relationships. One example is the famous paper on "sin" stocks, which provides evidence that stocks shunned by many investors (tobacco, alcohol, and gambling stocks) earn higher returns than comparable stocks.[8] This matter has been reassessed recently, and a lot of the performance differentials previously identified *have* been claimed to be attributable to simply comparing equal-weighted portfolios to value-weighted portfolios, thereby partly measuring the well-known size effect. The design of the original study seems not that biased,[9] but this example illustrates that drawing conclusions based on empirical data requires a cautious approach.

Relation of ESG Performance to Other Factors

The second piece of research analyses the performance of an ESG-tilted global equity portfolio against a global benchmark.[10] One should keep in mind that the authors work for MSCI (an ESG data provider), which may influence the credibility of the findings. However, this work has at least one very interesting feature: It analyses portfolio performance using a risk/return model that includes a number of other factors empirically shown to drive stock returns (i.e., size and value), thereby providing a good insight into how much of the ESG portfolio performance is attributable to these factors. The findings from this analysis are very interesting:

- The ESG portfolio outperforms by 1.1% per annum; 0.76% of this performance is attributable to style factors, while 0.43% represents genuine stock-specific returns (with another −0.1% attributable to country and currency effects).

- The results for the individual styles indicate that stocks with higher ESG ratings tend to have lower stock-specific risks, come primarily from the mid-cap space, and tend to have a higher valuation.

This illustrates that a high degree of ESG performance is associated with other company characteristics but can also lead to stock-specific superior returns.

Evidence from ESG Funds

There are a large number of studies on the performance of ESG and SI funds compared with conventional peers.[11,12] Most studies show that the returns from sustainable funds do not significantly differ from those of conventional funds, leading to the conclusion that ESG funds at least do not lag their conventional peers in terms of risk-adjusted performance. So the question remains why it seems so difficult to transform the documented positive relationship between superior ESG performance and superior stock returns into an outperformance at the fund level.

There are several possible reasons for this:

- Fund returns also contain the results of fundamentals-driven stock picking, so they do not only show the impact of the ESG analysis used.

- Many studies cover the US market and include returns that date back in time considerably; therefore, their sustainable investment concepts could be "old-fashioned," with a focus on exclusions as well as more ethical aspects.

But overall the empirical findings present strong evidence that sustainable investing does not entail forgoing financial performance. It is therefore possible to have a positive impact, reduce reputational risks, and at the same time achieve decent returns.

Other Asset Classes

So far, the focus has been on equity investing as ESG data on stocks are more accessible and available for longer periods than other asset classes. As ESG data are often on a company level, they can also be used for corporate bonds, but performance analyses are much harder for this asset class. Yet, there is also a solid body of evidence that superior ESG performance is linked to better credit ratings and lower spreads.[13,14,15] For sovereign bonds, it has also been

Figure 1.   Summary of Findings of Academic Studies on the Link between ESG Performance and Financial Performance

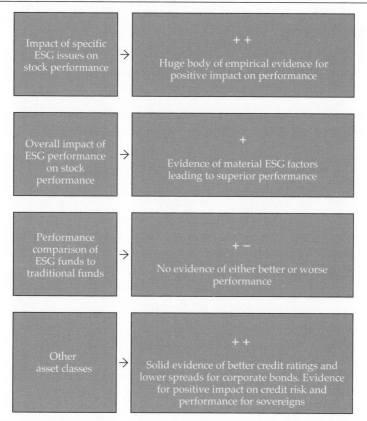

Source: LGT Capital Partners (2016).

documented that ESG performance positively influences both credit risk and performance.[16]

Summary

Overall, there is ample academic evidence that ESG parameters have a positive influence on the returns from financial assets (see **Figure 1**). Trying to translate these findings into superior portfolio performance leads to rather mixed results. Generally speaking, it is absolutely possible to create portfolios with superior ESG characteristics while achieving risk/return profiles that match those of traditional portfolios at the same time. There will presumably be more regulation to come with respect to ESG issues. This presents latent risks for entities with a poor ESG performance, which could face very tangible negative economic impacts. Incorporating a sound analysis of ESG factors into the investment process will therefore be in the best interest of investors, particularly with regard to their fiduciary duty to the ultimate asset owners.

Further Reading

- Clark, G. L., Feiner, A., & Viehs, M. (2015). *From the stockholder to the stakeholder: How sustainability can drive financial outperformance.* Available at SSRN 2508281.

- Fulton, M., Kahn, B. M., & Sharples, C. (2012). *Sustainable investing: Establishing long-term value and performance.* Available at SSRN 2222740.

- Kleine, J., Krautbauer, M., & Weller, T. (2013). *Nachhaltige Investments aus dem Blick der Wissenschaft: Leistungsversprechen und Realität, Analysebericht.* Research Center for Financial Services of Steinbeis-Hochschule Berlin, Berlin.

- Renneboog, L. D. R., Ter Horst, J. R., & Zhang, C. (2007). *Socially responsible investments: Methodology, risk and performance.* Center Discussion paper, 2007.

Endnotes

[1]Cremers, K. J., & Nair, V. B. (2005). Governance mechanisms and equity prices. *Journal of Finance, 60*(6), 2859–2894.

[2]Bauer, R., Guenster, N., & Otten, R. (2004). Empirical evidence on corporate governance in Europe: The effect on stock returns, firm value and performance. *Journal of Asset Management, 5*(2), 91–104.

[3]Dowell, G., Hart, S., & Yeung, B. (2000). Do corporate global environmental standards create or destroy market value? *Management Science, 46*(8), 1059–1074.

[4]Derwall, J., Gunster, N., Bauer, R., & Koedijk, K. (2004). The eco-efficiency premium puzzle. *Financial Analysts Journal, 61*(2), 51–63.

[5]Edmans, A. (2011). Does the stock market fully value intangibles? Employee satisfaction and equity prices. *Journal of Financial Economics, 101*(3), 621–640.

[6]Edmans, A., Li, L., & Zhang, C. (2014). *Employee satisfaction, labor market flexibility, and stock returns around the world*. (No. w20300). National Bureau of Economic Research.

[7]Khan, M., Serafeim, G., & Yoon, A. (2015). *Corporate sustainability: First evidence on materiality*. HBS Working paper 15–073.

[8]Hong, H., & Kacperczyk, M. (2009). The price of sin: The effects of social norms on markets. *Journal of Financial Economics, 93*(1), 15–36.

[9]Adamsson, H., & Hoepner, A. (2015). *The 'price of sin' aversion: Ivory tower or real investable alpha?* Working paper.

[10]Nagy, Z., Kassam, A., & Lee, L. (2015). *Can ESG add alpha? An analysis of ESG tilt and momentum strategies*. MSCI Research paper.

[11]Statman, M. (2000). Socially responsible mutual funds (corrected). *Financial Analysts Journal, 56*(3), 30–39.

[12]Seitz, J. (2010). *Nachhaltige Investments: eine empirisch-vergleichende Analyse der Performance ethisch-nachhaltiger Investmentfonds in Europa*. Hamburg: Diplomica Verlag.

[13]Klock, M. S., Mansi, S. A., & Maxwell, W. F. (2005). Does corporate governance matter to bondholders? *Journal of Financial and Quantitative Analysis, 40*(4), 693–719.

[14]Bauer, R., Derwall, J., & Hann, D. (2009). *Employee relations and credit risk*. Available at SSRN 1483112.

[15]Bauer, R., & Hann, D. (2010). *Corporate environmental management and credit risk*. Available at SSRN 1660470.

[16]Kohut, J., & Beeching, A. (2013). *Sovereign bonds: Spotlight on ESG risks*. PRI Report.

5. Development of the Regulatory and Legislative Environment for Sustainable Investment

Dr. Agnes Neher
Sustainability Manager, Bank J. Safra Sarasin

Overview of the Regulatory Landscape

European markets have developed very differently regarding hard regulation in the field of sustainable investment. Although around 13 European countries have some kind of regulation in place (see **Figure 2**), the scope of legislation is quite different. Some countries focus mainly on mandatory disclosure by pension funds, such as Austria, Germany, or Spain. Other countries, like Sweden, France, or the Netherlands, go one step further. These countries have additional rules in place prohibiting the financing of weapons or the mandatory consideration of environmental, social, and governance (ESG) issues in the investment process by state pension funds.

Besides hard laws, there are also a variety of soft or voluntary regulations in place,[2] such as the Swiss Code of Best Practice for Corporate Governance. Furthermore, there are basic self-regulation initiatives, such as the Principles for Responsible Investment (PRI). This international network of investors puts its six principles into practice and supports (amongst other activities) its signatories' implementation. In 2014, the network started the PRI Montreal Carbon Pledge to commit investors to measure and publicly disclose the carbon footprint of their investment portfolios on an annual basis.[3] In addition, there are international initiatives putting external pressure on investors by campaigning or engaging with governments or other policymakers, amongst others. One of the most active initiatives in this field is ShareAction, which claims to "exist to make investment a force for good."[4]

Current Regulation in France, the Netherlands, and the United Kingdom

Several countries have implemented hard legislation in the field of sustainable investment. These regulatory approaches differ both in size and format. France, the Netherlands, and the UK have overall the greatest number and extent of legislation in Europe. This corresponds to the size and development of sustainable investment in these countries relative to their European

Figure 2.   Hard Regulatory Approaches in EU Countries and Switzerland

■ Countries with regulatory approaches
■ Countries without regulatory approaches

Source: Neher (2015).[1]

neighbours. According to Eurosif, the UK is, for example, a flourishing and leading market in sustainable finance.[5] The most salient laws in France, the Netherlands, and the UK are presented in the following section.

France. France has a variety of laws in the field of sustainable investment that target pension funds, state pension funds, and investment companies. These can be seen in **Table 1**. Just recently the amendment of Article 173 of the French Energy Transition Law came into effect on January 2016. It requires French investors to fully disclose details of their investment policies,

Table 1. Regulatory Approaches in France, the Netherlands, UK, and Switzerland[6]

Country	Year	Legislation	Type of Legislation	Explanation
France	2001	Employee Savings Plans (*La loi Fabius*)	Hard law	Mandatory requirement for investors to disclose in their annual reports the extent to which they take ESG indicators into account when buying or selling stocks and securities and when exercising their shareholder rights, amongst other requirements
	2005/2008	*Fonds de Réserve pour les Retraites* (FRR)	Hard law	Introduction of a sustainable investment strategy and mandatory inclusion of at least one *fond solidaire*
	2010/2012	The second *Grenelle Law* (Grenelle II)	Hard law	Public disclosure of open-ended investment companies and investment management companies (fund managers) about how they integrate ESG objectives in their investment decisions, first on their websites and then in their annual reports
	2015	Amendment of *Article 173 of the French Energy Transition Law*	Hard law	Mandatory climate disclosure of institutional investors
The Netherlands	1995	*Green Investment Directive*	Hard law	Tax reduction for green investments, such as wind and solar energy or organic farming
	2008/2013	*Pension Fund Act*	Hard law	Enhancing the overall governance of pension funds; for example, the pension fund must publicly disclose details of its sustainable investment strategy
	2013	*Law against financing of landmines and cluster munitions*	Hard law	Exclusion of investments in landmines and cluster munitions

(continued)

Table 1. Regulatory Approaches in France, the Netherlands, UK, and Switzerland[6] (continued)

Country	Year	Legislation	Type of Legislation	Explanation
UK	1995/2001	Amendments to the 1995 Pensions Act. Sustainable Investment Pensions Disclosure Regulation	Hard law	Public requirement for pension funds to state in the Statement of Investment Principles the extent to which (if at all) social, environmental, and ethical considerations are taken into account in the selection, retention, and realisation of investments
	2000	Trustee Act	Hard law	Ensuring that investments made by charities are compatible with their stated aims, including applying ethical considerations to investments
	2003	Community Investment Tax Relief (CITR)	Hard law	Encouragement of investments in disadvantaged communities
	2010	UK Stewardship Code	Hard law for UK-regulated asset managers[7]; soft regulation for asset managers, asset owners, and service providers	Set of good corporate governance for investors' engagement with companies, issued by the Financial Reporting Council
Switzerland	2013	The revised version of the Swiss Federal Act on War Materials	Hard law	Prohibition of the production, trade, and storage of controversial weapons as well as financing of and investing in such enterprises
	2002/2014	Swiss Code of Best Practice for Corporate Governance	Soft regulation	Set of good corporate governance for companies, including the Guidelines for Institutional Investors to practice voting rights, issued by economiesuisse
	2014	VegüV/Minder Initiative	Hard law	Set of voting obligations that institutional investors have to meet, amongst others

Source: Based on Neher (2015).[8]

their carbon footprint, and their alignment with climate goals, and it obliges them to report on climate risks.

The Netherlands. The Netherlands was one of the first countries to put in place legislation regarding sustainable investment. The newest law against the financing of landmines and cluster munitions, from 2013, forbids financial institutions to invest in producers of such weapons.[9]

United Kingdom. The UK is a common law[10] country, like the USA. Its sustainable investment market has been developed similarly to those countries involved in the early sustainability movements, such as the anti–Vietnam War campaigns in the USA.[11] The UK's commitment to sustainability is particularly striking with laws in place that promote pension fund disclosures, charity investment strategies, and tax relief for community investing, as can be seen in Table 1.

Current Regulation in Switzerland

Switzerland's regulatory landscape regarding sustainable investment is fairly straightforward. In 2002, legal changes were made that require funds to establish rules on shareholder rights. Although funds do not have to participate in proxy voting, the step can be seen as a legal basis for shareholder engagement.[12] In 2014, VegüV (Verordnung gegen übermässige Vergütungen bei börsenkotierten Aktiengesellschaften), generally known as the Minder Initiative, came into force. Under this new law, shareholders received more rights in determining the management's remuneration. For example, companies must allow shareholders to vote at annual shareholder meetings on the remuneration for members of the board of directors. Under this law, pension funds are required to exercise their right to vote concerning the remuneration of the board.[13] In 2013, Switzerland introduced a revised version of the Swiss Federal Act on War Materials. The new version of the law explicitly forbids the production, trade, and storage of controversial weapons as well as investing in such enterprises if used as a substitute for direct financing. Cluster bombs— together with atomic, biological, and chemical (ABC) weapons as well as anti-personnel mines—all fall under the category of controversial weapons.

Looking at guidelines in the field of sustainable investment, the Swiss Code of Best Practice for Corporate Governance, including the Guidelines for institutional investors to practice voting rights from the Swiss Business Federation economiesuisse, merits particular attention. Since its revision in 2014, the Code—which mainly targets listed Swiss companies—points out that sustainability positively influences the long-term return of a company.

The additional Guidelines include five principles for institutional investors to meet their responsibilities when practicing their proxy voting rights.[14]

Dynamic International Developments

On the international level, two important developments in the sustainable investment market can be highlighted. The first is the work of the Task Force on Climate-Related Financial Disclosures (TCFD), a task force commissioned by the Financial Stability Board (FSB), with its recently published disclosure framework. The second noteworthy initiative is the founding of the High-Level Expert Group (HLEG) on Sustainable Finance by the European Commission (EC). The TCFD recommendations framework aims to improve and increase climate-related financial disclosures by aligning the disclosure of companies regarding climate change risks with investors' needs.[15] In comparison, the European Expert Group was commissioned to advise on the development of a comprehensive European sustainable finance strategy. This should be done through the integration of "sustainability considerations into its financial policy framework in order to mobilise finance for sustainable growth."[16] In June 2017, the HLEG published its interim report, which identifies key areas in the financial system where adjustments are needed to reach this repositioning, such as defining unified sustainability taxonomy and adjusting existing frameworks to better address sustainable investing.[17] A full report is expected to be released at the end of 2017.

Fiduciary Duty

Pension funds investing sustainably often fear they may violate their fiduciary duty when adopting sustainable investment policies. Fiduciary duties[18] are "imposed upon a person who exercises some discretionary power in the interests of another person in circumstances that give rise to a relationship of trust and confidence."[19] In 2005, Freshfields Bruckhaus Deringer published the report "A Legal Framework for the Integration of Environment, Social and Governance Issues into Institutional Investment." This report examined, on behalf of the UNEP Finance Initiative (UNEP FI), how the integration of sustainability criteria is compatible with the fiduciary duty of pension fund officials. After an analysis of jurisdictions in ten countries, the report concludes, "the integration of ESG considerations into an investment analysis so as to more reliably predict financial performance is clearly permissible and is arguably required in all jurisdictions."[20,21] Just recently, in September 2015, the UNEP FI published in cooperation with the United Global Compact, the PRI, and the UNEP Inquiry the new report "Fiduciary Duty in the

21st Century." After conducting structured interviews with 50 asset owners, investment managers, lawyers, and regulators from eight countries, the study concludes that "[i]ntegrating ESG issues into investment [...] will enable investors to make better investment decisions and improve investment performance consistent with their fiduciary duty."[22] These market-relevant studies thus confirm that integrating ESG issues into investment processes is consistent with the fiduciary duty of investors, especially asset owners, if not a requirement. In line with this conclusion, the HLEG also included in their recommendations that the EC clarify that fiduciary duty encompasses managing sustainability risks.[23]

Conclusion

Different developments of regulatory approaches in the field of sustainable investment have been observed in Europe and internationally. Also, the UN COP21 climate change conference in November 2015 closed with the adoption of the Paris Agreement proposal by the president. The unprecedented universal agreement to reduce global greenhouse gas emissions to net zero by 2050 will force regulators to introduce new legislation in different fields. According to responsible-investor.com (2015), "the voice of institutional investors has been louder than ever before" in Paris.[24] There are several text sections that reflect the strong and central role of institutional investors at the conference. Time will show what the agreement means for institutional investors in the European sustainable investment market.

Further Reading

- Hebb, T., Hawley, J. P., Hoepner, A. G. F., Neher, A. L., & Wood, D. (2015). *The Routledge Handbook of Responsible Investment*. New York: Routledge.

- RI Insight. (2015). *Switzerland: Sustainable finance the Helvetic way*. Available at: https://www.responsible-investor.com//images/uploads/reports/RI_Insight_Switzerland.pdf.

- UN PRI. (2017). *Global ESG regulatory mapping*. Available at: https://www.unpri.org/page/responsible-investment-regulation.

Endnotes

[1]See Neher, A. (2015).

[2]Hard law—as opposed to soft regulation—refers to legally binding obligations that are precise. Soft regulation refers to a wide range of quasi-legal instruments, such as guidelines or codes. These lack immediate, uniformly binding, direct effects or precision. For more information, please refer to Neher, A. (2015). *ESG risks and Responsible Investment in financial markets*. Metropolis, Weimar b. Marburg.

[3]PRI Montreal Carbon Pledge. (2015). Available at: http://montrealpledge.org/.

[4]ShareAction. (2017). *About us.* Available at: http://www.shareaction.org/about.

[5]Eurosif. (2016). *European SRI study.* Available at: http://www.eurosif.org/wp-content/uploads/2016/11/SRI-study-2016-HR.pdf.

[6]This is only a selection of the main laws in the countries and is not exhaustive.

[7]UK asset managers have to report using the regulatory approach "comply or explain." Rather than setting down binding laws, the UK government sets out the Code that UK-regulated asset managers may either comply with, or if they do not comply, explain publicly why they do not.

[8]See Neher, A. (2015).

[9]European Fund and Asset Management Association. (2014). *Report on Responsible Investment.* Available at: http://www.efama.org/Publications/Public/Responsible_Investment/140228_Responsible_Investment_Report_online.pdf.

[10]For further distinction in the development of sustainable investment between common law and civil law countries, please refer to Hebb, T., Hawley, J. P., Hoepner, A. G., Wood, D., & Neher, A. (2015). *The Routledge Handbook of Responsible Investment.* New York: Routledge.

[11]Ibid.

[12]Neher, A. (2015). "Responsible Investment in Austria, Germany and Switzerland." In Hebb et al. (ed.), *The Routledge Handbook of Responsible Investment.* New York: Routledge.

[13]For further information, please refer to the Federal Council, https://www.admin.ch/opc/de/classified-compilation/20132519/index.html.

[14]See also economiesuisse. (2016). *Swiss Code of Best Practice for Corporate Governance.* Available at: http://www.economiesuisse.ch/de/publikationen/swiss-code-best-practice-corporate-governance-english. And economiesuisse. (2013). *Guidelines for institutional investors governing the exercising of participation rights in public limited companies.* Available at: https://www.icgn.org/sites/default/files/LD_130121_E.pdf.

[15]For further information, please refer to the TCFD, https://www.fsb-tcfd.org/.

[16]European Commission (2017). *Sustainable finance.* Available at: https://ec.europa.eu/info/business-economy-euro/banking-and-finance/sustainable-finance_en#towards-an-eu-strategy-on-sustainable-finance.

[17]For further information, please refer to "Financing a Sustainable European Economy." Available at: https://ec.europa.eu/info/sites/info/files/170713-sustainable-finance-report_en.pdf.

[18]Specific fiduciary duties are "duty of loyalty," the "duty of care," and the "duty of impartiality."

[19]Freshfields Bruckhaus Deringer. (2005). *A legal framework for the integration of environmental, social and governance issues into institutional investment.* Written for the Asset Management Working Group of the UNEP Finance Initiative. Available at: http://www.unepfi.org/fileadmin/documents/freshfields_legal_resp_20051123.pdf, p.8.

[20]Ibid.

[21]It has to be added that the law firm (Freshfields Bruckhaus Deringer) assumes that the specific sustainable investment must have passed the process "taking ESG consideration into account" that it has built. For further information, please refer to the report.

[22]UN Global Compact, UNEP FI, PRI. (2015). *Fiduciary duty in the 21st century.* Available at: http://www.unepfi.org/fileadmin/documents/fiduciary_duty_21st_century.pdf, p. 10.

[23]The High-Level Expert Group. (2017). *Financing a sustainable European economy.* Available at: https://ec.europa.eu/info/sites/info/files/170713-sustainable-finance-report_en.pdf, p.22ff.

[24]responsible-investor.com. (2015). *COP 21 Wrap-up: The voice of institutional investors has been louder than ever before.* Available at: https://www.responsible-investor.com/home/article/cop21_the_voice_of_institutional_investors/.

Part 2: Different Approaches to Sustainable Investment and Specific Asset Classes

6. Introduction to Different Approaches to Sustainable Investment

There is a huge selection of products and services available to anyone looking to invest in a sustainable way. The advantage of such a broad offering is that solutions can be found for virtually all requirements and asset classes. The only drawback is that it is both difficult and time-consuming to gain an overview of the many different approaches and then identify the one that best suits one's organisation.

The purpose of this Handbook is to make this step much easier for institutional investors in particular. Parts 2 and 3 provide a description and explanation of practically all forms of sustainable investment currently available in the market. Their pros and cons are highlighted, and references are provided for further reading.

Part 2 is organised as follows:

- Chapters 7–13 present different approaches to sustainable investment.

- Chapters 14–18 explore specific sustainable asset classes.

Part 3 supplements this with the following themes:

- Chapters 19–20 deal with interdisciplinary topics relating to different asset classes and approaches.

So, what relevance do these many approaches and themes have for different portfolios? Based on the asset classes commonly found in the portfolios of institutional investors, **Table 2** shows which approaches are particularly suitable for which asset classes. The relevance of interdisciplinary topics for certain asset classes is also highlighted. This table illustrates that not all approaches can be combined with all asset classes. For certain asset classes, such as actively managed equities and bonds, the market for sustainable investments is very mature and offers many different investment solutions. For other asset classes, such as passive investment strategies or commodities, investment solutions are available but there are fewer options than for other asset classes. There are also combinations that do not make sense from a logical or technical viewpoint and are therefore labelled as "not applicable."

Taking one's portfolio and the asset classes it contains as a starting point, Table 2 can help identify which approaches come into question for a particular organisation and which other themes might be relevant.

Table 2. Relevance of Different Approaches for Different Asset Classes

🔲 High relevance 🔲 Medium relevance ⬛ Low/no relevance ☐ not applicable

	Chapter		Equities active	Equities passive ①	Corporate bonds active	Corporate bonds passive ①	Sovereign bonds	Real estate (direct)	Private Equity	Other alternatives ②
Approaches	7	Exclusion criteria	Medium	Medium	Medium	Medium	Medium	Low	Medium	Medium ⑩
	8	Best-in-class approach	Medium	Medium ⑤	Medium	Medium	Medium	Medium	Low	Low
	9	ESG integration approach	Medium	Low	Low	Low	Low	Medium	Medium	Low
	10, 11	Active voting/Shareholder engagement	Medium	Medium	Low	Low	Low	Medium	Medium	Low
	12	Sustainable thematic investments	Medium	Medium ⑥	Low ⑧	Low	Low	Low	Low	Low ⑪
	13	Impact investing/Investments for Development ③						Low	Medium	Medium ⑫
Sustainable asset classes	14	Green bonds			Medium	Low	Medium			Low
	15	Sustainable infrastructure investments	Medium ④	Low	Medium ⑧	Low	Medium	Low ⑧	Medium	Medium
	16	Sustainable private-equity investments							Medium	
	17	Sustainable real estate investments	Low					Medium		
	18	Integrating sustainability into commodity investing								Low

(continued)

Table 2. Relevance of Different Approaches for Different Asset Classes (continued)

	Chapter	Equities active	Equities passive ① ⑦	Corporate bonds active ⑨	Corporate bonds passive ①	Sovereign bonds	Real estate (direct)	Private Equity	Other alternatives ② ⑬
Cross-sectional themes	19	Climate change and associated risks for investors							
	20	The role of indices in sustainable investing							

Comments on individual cells

① In the case of sustainable investments, passive investments are actually "semi-passive" as they mostly incorporate an active selection based on sustainability criteria, which is then modelled in a passively managed product. By its very nature, however, this product deviates from traditional indices (see also chapter 20).

② Hedge funds, commodity investments, private bonds

③ Investments for Development are a form of impact investing. These are, by far, the most important form of this investment approach in Switzerland

④ Refers to listed infrastructure companies or funds (e.g., so-called "yield cos")

⑤ Investments in sustainability indices based on a best-in-class approach provide a "semi-passive" approach. By their very nature, however, such indices tend to show a deviation versus standard benchmarks.

⑥ E.g. water exchange traded funds (ETFs), climate ETFs. But same restriction as mentioned under (5)

⑦ E.g. climate ETFs. But same restriction as mentioned under (5)

⑧ Possible through investments in green bonds issued by companies or governments

⑨ This does not refer to green bonds, but to the consideration of climate risks when assessing and selecting corporate or sovereign bonds

⑩ E.g. exclusion of soft commodities (agri futures, etc.) or hedge funds in general

⑪ E.g. investments in gold with a sustainability certificate

⑫ Typical form: private bonds (the most commonly used instrument in microfinance, for example)

⑬ CAT bonds or insurance products for climate risks can play a role here

General comments

— The table takes into consideration whether products in the combinations specified are available in the market

— "Positive screening," a term sometimes used in connection with sustainable investments, is counted here as "best-in-class" rather than a separate approach.

Source: Swiss Sustainable Finance (2016).[1,2]

On this basis, Part 2 can be used as a reference work: Readers need study only the chapters that are relevant for their own portfolios. Technical terms are not defined in each chapter, but important terms are explained in a short glossary at the end of the Handbook. A more-detailed glossary is provided on the SSF website, where it is regularly updated and extended.[3]

One important dimension is not integrated into this table: What is the motivation for sustainable investment? Depending on the institutional investor's ultimate objective, different combinations make more sense. Prioritising combinations according to objective and motivation is dealt with in chapter 22 (Implementing a Sustainable Investment Policy—A Practical Guide), in Part 4. Part 4 of the Handbook also provides practical tips and concrete instructions for defining and implementing a sustainable investment policy from the perspective of different investor types. Part 4 is intended as a sort of recipe book to help investors identify and progressively implement a solution that works for them.

Endnotes

[1] The weighting of the different strategies was determined by the editorial team and was based on estimates by experts and asset owner representatives.

[2] Swiss Sustainable Finance & University of Zurich. (2016). *Swiss investments for a better world.* Available at: http://www.sustainablefinance.ch/upload/cms/user/SSF_A4_Layout_RZ-1.pdf.

[3] http://www.sustainablefinance.ch/en/glossary-_content---1--3077.html.

7. Exclusions

Jonathan Horlacher, CFA
Financial Analyst, Credit Suisse (Switzerland)

Antonios Koutsoukis, CFA
Financial Analyst, Credit Suisse (Switzerland)

The exclusion approach (also known as negative screening) refers to the deliberate exclusion of industries, business activities, or products from an investment portfolio based on values, ethics, or principles. Typically, investors define a set of exclusion criteria and apply these through negative screening, either on their existing assets or as part of individual investment decisions. There are two main types of exclusion approaches: unconditional exclusions of business activities incompatible with the investor's values (values-based screening/exclusions) and conditional exclusions of companies based on breaches of certain global ESG standards, such as UN Global Compact or ILO conventions (norms-based screening/exclusions). The former is currently by far the most established and widely used approach to sustainable investing: In 2016, USD15.0 trillion, or 17% of total managed assets, applied a values-based exclusion screen according to the Global Sustainable Investing Alliance (GSIA).[1] In Switzerland, investment portfolios worth several hundred billion CHF apply some sort of screens that go beyond the legally required exclusions (i.e., internationally banned weapons).[2] The more complex norms-based screening approach is applied to USD6.2 trillion globally, most of which are European assets, and CHF164 billion in Switzerland. Exclusion approaches often represent a starting point for institutional investors on which more complex forms of sustainable investing build. In some cases (such as anti-personnel mines), exclusions can even be legally required in certain jurisdictions, including Switzerland (see also chapter 5 on regulatory requirements).

Ethics, Values, and Investment Objectives

The decision to deliberately not invest in certain industries opens up a debate due to conflicting priorities. On the one hand, any trust or pension fund has the fiduciary duty to pursue the best possible financial performance for its beneficiaries; on the other hand, broader social and environmental concerns are increasingly also taken into account. Early examples of exclusion include the divestment campaigns against the Apartheid regime in South Africa in the 1980s or against tobacco firms in the 1990s. Over time, other controversies have arisen, such as genetically modified organisms (GMOs) or carbon emissions. Coal companies are the latest target of a divestment campaign, led mainly by US universities. The full list of controversies also includes the widely applied exclusion screens on "vices," such as alcohol, adult entertainment, gambling, and weapons as well as more-specific issues, such as nuclear energy, animal testing, stem cells, or agrochemicals. As cultural norms vary across countries, some controversies can be very prominent in some countries but non-existent in others. Topics such as nuclear energy and genetically modified organisms are much more of an issue in Europe than in the United States, while pornography and gambling are less shunned by European investors. In Switzerland, the top three exclusion criteria listed in the latest market study were human rights violations, labour rights violations, and corruption and bribery.[3]

There are two main reasons for institutional investors to apply exclusion strategies. The historically important and more obvious reason is a clear mandate to exclude a certain activity regardless of financial considerations. A clear mandate can arise from:

- a moral stance and the nature of the institution/reflection of investors' values (e.g., directly conflicting with certain industries);

- legal or regulatory restrictions (e.g., production of weapons banned by international law, such as anti-personnel mines or cluster bombs); or

- instructions/pressure from beneficiaries/asset owners.

The second, less obvious reason to exclude stems from financial considerations is that if an industry is expected to significantly lose value in the future due to ongoing controversies, tougher regulation, or consumer boycotts, it might make sense to divest even from a purely financial viewpoint. But as it turns out, the financial case is not as clear-cut as one might think.

Effects of Exclusions

Negative screening, depending on the severity of criteria, can potentially impose investment constraints on investors. Some of the globally most typical exclusion criteria are listed in **Table 3**. If the exclusion is limited to companies with considerable sales exposure (above 5%) to a common set of controversial businesses, the investment universe is reduced by approximately 9% (see example based on MSCI World in Table 3).

Depending on the type and severity of the exclusion criteria set by investors, the opportunity cost of divesting stocks can be substantial, especially with values-based exclusion approaches. Companies with exposure to controversial business areas, such as alcohol, tobacco, and gambling, have

Table 3.   **Excluded Percentage of MSCI World per Exclusion Criteria (based on 2016 MSCI World weights)**

Controversial Business Involvement	Any Involvement	>5% Revenues	>10% Revenues
Landmines and cluster bombs	0.6%	N/A	N/A
Weapons and defense	8.3%	1.9%	1.2%
Firearms	0.8%	0.0%	0.0%
Alcohol	14.7%	2.6%	1.9%
Tobacco	8.6%	2.0%	1.8%
Gambling	3.5%	0.5%	0.5%
Adult entertainment	6.0%	0.0%	0.0%
Nuclear energy	6.5%	1.7%	1.3%
Coal	1.7%	N/A	0.1%
Animal testing: medical	13.2%	3.1%	If not AAALAC accredited
Animal testing: non-medical	12.7%	9.4%	If not AAALAC accredited
GMO	2.3%	0.7%	0.6%
Embryonic stem cells	10.0%	N/A	N/A
All criteria combined	**47.4%**	**9.0%**	**7.1%**

Notes: Sales exposures not applicable to some criteria such as landmines or stem cells. In the case of animal testing, AAALAC accreditation is used as mitigating factor for exposed companies. Combined figures include animal testing for any involvement, but not in restricted totals.
Sources: MSCI, Datastream, Credit Suisse (2016).

outperformed the S&P 1200 Global benchmark by almost 2.7% annually over the last 10 years.[4] Even on a risk-adjusted basis, this group fared better than the broader index in this period. A benchmark that excludes all companies with controversial business exposures underperformed by 0.8% annually. The excluded companies tend to be larger and less risky than the typical stock in the S&P 1200 Global, which results in portfolios with different factor exposures (see also chapter 4 on performance). However, when limiting the exclusions with a sales threshold or to categories with a minimal weight in the global market, there is no significant performance difference. For example, screening out controversial weapons, representing just 0.6% of the MSCI World, has had no negative effect on the performance of a portfolio, as illustrated by the chart of the MSCI World ex Controversial Weapons compared to the regular index (see **Figure 3**).

In the case of a norms-based exclusion approach, the effect on performance is neutral to positive, since red-flagged companies represent just a

Figure 3. **MSCI World ex Controversial Weapons vs. MSCI World**

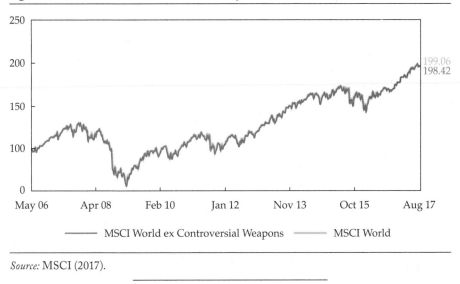

Source: MSCI (2017).

small part of the overall universe (specifically 3%, see **Figure 4**), while such exclusions are also commonly assumed to reduce downside risks.

How to Mitigate the Financial Impact of Exclusions

All too-extensive values-based exclusions can lead to a negative impact on performance. However, there are ways to limit the impact of a restricted investment universe. These include reviewing risk/return objectives so that they are fully aligned with the ESG guidelines, portfolio optimisation, and constructing ESG strategies that help generate alpha.

1. Careful definition of ESG guidelines. When first defining the ESG policy, a foundation or pension fund board should take into account the following factors:

- Main values and objectives of the organisation (i.e., if a foundation is focused on supporting research on lung cancer, it will most likely want to avoid investments in tobacco companies; if a pension fund represents public sector employees, it might want to avoid investing in companies that violate international norms ratified by its country).

- Reputational risk (a large public sector investor in the focus of NGOs and media might want to avoid investing in very controversial companies that violate human rights and environmental standards).

Figure 4. Distribution of the MSCI World Universe into Four Different Norm-Based Rating Levels

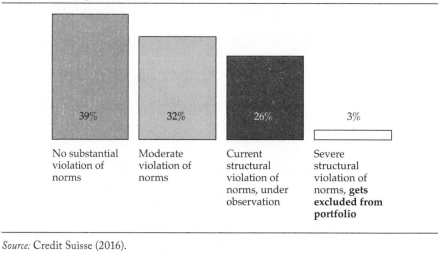

No substantial violation of norms — 39%

Moderate violation of norms — 32%

Current structural violation of norms, under observation — 26%

Severe structural violation of norms, **gets excluded from portfolio** — 3%

Source: Credit Suisse (2016).

- Effect on portfolio (the investment universe of an investor mainly investing in Swiss markets might not be affected by the exclusion of coal companies).

Including detailed information on the factors named above helps to define a set of exclusion criteria matching the values of the organisation, while reducing potential reputational and financial risks and limiting restrictions on portfolio management.

2. Portfolio optimisation. In case an approach with a considerable effect on the investment universe is chosen, the divergence between the investment universe and the benchmark can be reduced through optimisation. This can reduce the impact of unintended bets that arise due to the difference between stock weights in the benchmark and the divested portfolio. For example, companies exposed to controversial businesses tend to have higher dividend yields, price-to-book values, and market capitalisation than non-exposed companies. Excluding them can alter a portfolio's exposure to these factors. Optimisation of the non-controversial businesses universe can lead to better performance. In practice, optimisation does not always work as intended, because the sensitivity of a portfolio to a factor (such as its beta) can change over time. From the investor's viewpoint, this means that portfolios must be reviewed and rebalanced frequently.

3. Generating alpha with ESG. An alternative method of offsetting the effect of a constrained universe is by constructing outperforming strategies based on other sustainable investment strategies. Investors can partly offset the effect of a smaller stock universe through a more careful selection of the underlying securities, and more specifically by focusing on companies with potential for improvement (see chapters 4, 8, 9, and 12 for more information). The vast majority of studies find a positive impact on financial performance by including ESG-specific information into the asset selection process, as documented in a meta-study by Arabesque Asset Management and the University of Oxford in 2015.[5]

Conclusion

Exclusion screening is a well-established sustainable investment approach applied by some of the largest asset owners, such as the Norwegian Government Pension Fund.[6] This allows them to apply their specific sustainability concept and value set to their investment strategy. A sensible set of exclusion criteria is based on a certain materiality threshold, as the impact on the investment universe can be severe with absolute exclusions. With an exposure threshold based, for instance, on sales figures, exclusion screening does not lead to a diminished financial performance. To achieve this, exclusion guidelines have to be defined carefully and mitigating factors need to be considered in portfolio construction. Furthermore, investors can combine exclusion screening with other ESG approaches to enhance the sustainability and financial potential of their investment portfolios.

Further Reading

- Clark, G. L., Feiner, A., & Viehs, M. (2015). *From the stockholder to the stakeholder: How sustainability can drive financial outperformance.* Available at: https://papers.ssrn.com/sol3/papers.cfm?abstract_id=2508281.

- Hong, H., & Kacperczyk, M. (2009). The price of sin: The effects of social norms on markets. *Journal of Financial Economics*, *93*(1), 15–36. Available at: http://pages.stern.nyu.edu/~sternfin/mkacperc/public_html/sin.pdf.

- Statman, M., & Glushkov, D. (2009). The wages of social responsibility. *Financial Analysts Journal*, *65*(4), 33–46. Available at: http://www.cfapubs.org/doi/abs/10.2469/faj.v65.n4.5.

Endnotes

[1]Global Sustainable Investment Alliance. (2016). *Global sustainable investment review 2016.* Available at: www.gsi-alliance.org.

[2]Forum Nachhaltige Geldanlagen, Swiss Sustainable Finance. (2017). *Sustainable investment in Switzerland—Excerpt from the sustainable investment market report 2017.*

[3]Ibid.

[4]For more information, see Hong and Kacperczyk (2009) or Statman and Glushkov (2009).

[5]Clark, G. L., Feiner, A., & Viehs, M. (2015). *From the stockholder to the stakeholder: How sustainability can drive financial outperformance.* Smith School of Enterprise and the Environment.

[6]Norges Bank Investment Management. (2016). *Observation and exclusion of companies.* Available at: https://www.nbim.no/en/responsibility/exclusion-of-companies/.

Case Study: Velux Foundation

A foundation increases its impact through sustainable investment.

Information on the organisation	
Type of organisation	Charitable foundation
Assets under management (as of 31.12.2016)	CHF210 million
Approximate asset allocation (as of 31.12.2016)	**Asset allocation by asset class:** CHF bonds: 19% Foreign currency bonds: 28% Swiss equities: 8% Global equities: 35% Real estate: 5% Others: 5% **Asset allocation by region:** Switzerland: 27% Global: 73%
Information on sustainable investment policy	
Who initiated the drafting of a sustainable investment policy?	The initiative for considering sustainability aspects in investment activity came from the Managing Director. The Board of Trustees were rather sceptical to start with, due to concerns about potential effects on costs and performance.
What was the main motivation for this step?	The main motivation was to make investments that would significantly enhance, rather than impair, the effects of the Foundation's funding activity. The discussion was triggered by a concrete example: In 2005, the Foundation financed a wind project in Madagascar as part of its donation activities. At the same time, it was invested in several companies that were entangled in various environmental catastrophes in Africa. The Managing Director felt it was a zero-sum game to use dividends earned from these oil companies to finance renewable energy projects on the same continent. This prompted a discussion in the Board of Trustees about how to avoid such contradictions. Another reason for defining a sustainable investment policy was the consideration that investments made by a tax-exempt foundation should not conflict with international norms.
What are the main components/content of the sustainable investment policy?	The investment policy contains the following wording: Investments may only be made in companies that uphold the principles of the UN Global Compact, a business code of conduct on such issues as human rights, working conditions, the environment, and corruption. Compliance with these principles is verified every year.

	In 2017, "Thematic Impact Investments" were added to the policy. The Board of Trustees decided to invest 10% of the Foundation's assets by 2020 in accordance with its purpose (i.e., measures to combat climate change). Additionally, a decision was taken to implement a carbon divestment strategy by 2020.
How was the sustainable investment policy implemented?	The Foundation manages its assets by granting mandates to third parties. An initial review of portfolios by the Bank Sarasin revealed that few securities had an inadequate sustainability rating. Discussions were subsequently held with portfolio managers to work towards selling such investments. Simultaneously, when granting new mandates, the Investment Committee consistently considered how sustainability aspects were incorporated during the investment process (even if this was not yet one of the investment policy's explicit criteria). No compromises whatsoever were made regarding performance or costs. As a result of this approach, 60% of all assets were already managed in a sustainable manner by 2014.
	Based on the experiences gained and the discussions in the Board of Trustees, a commitment to adhere to the Global Compact was formally adopted as part of the investment policy in 2014. After that, discussions were sought with all asset managers to ensure that this new guideline was also modelled in existing mandates. For most of them, there was no problem integrating this criterion into their investment activity; for those managers not willing or able to do so, the mandate was cancelled. An annual screening of the mandates is performed. Investments that do not comply with the guidelines must be sold within three months.
	Thematic impact investments are implemented through illiquid private equity, infrastructure, or real estate investments.
What resources have been deployed for this?	The Managing Director drafted and implemented the sustainable investment policy. In certain phases, he also drew on external support. A consultant supported him when selecting the research provider and checking whether external asset managers can meet the new criterion. CSSP handles the annual review of all portfolios.
What were your experiences with the policy implementation?	It was certainly a very long process. Discussions in the Board of Trustees took a lot of time due to the differences in values and opinions. On top of that, knowledge on sustainable investments was still fairly limited when the discussions began in 2005, and the public debate had barely started. The Investment Committee's high degree of autonomy facilitated a gradual expansion of sustainable investments, even without formally adopting a sustainable investment policy.
What were notable difficulties?	It was not easy to meet the conditions that sustainable investment should not result in higher costs, undermine performance, or increase risk exposure. Communicating the necessity and priority of a sustainable investment strategy was also a challenge.
What do you consider to be the main benefits of your sustainable investment policy?	The current investments made by the tax-exempt, charitable Foundation are consistent with the Foundation's mandate, and this helps to optimise its impact.

8. Best-in-Class Approach

Bernard de Halleux
Head of Candriam Switzerland LLC, Candriam Investors Group

Ben Peeters
Senior Investment Specialist SRI, Candriam Investors Group

What Is a Best-in-Class Approach?

In contrast to the exclusion approach, whereby certain industries are ruled out for being detrimental to a sustainable economy, the best-in-class approach is more pragmatic and follows a less black-and-white approach: It prioritises best practices of companies, regardless of their respective industry.

The best-in-class approach gives investors a holistic view of companies' commitment to sustainability. For this approach to be effective, the companies must be analysed from both a macro- and micro-economic point of view, meaning that:

- First, investors need to identify which companies are best placed to tackle the major challenges of sustainable development, namely climate change, the over-exploitation of natural resources, demographic changes, health, and well-being. This macro-economic analysis must be performed for every industry because certain industries (e.g., mining) are significantly more exposed to the issue of natural resources, for example, than the banking industry.

- At the same time, investors need to consider micro-economic issues related to how a company manages the interests of its stakeholders (including customers, suppliers, local communities, and employees) from an ESG perspective.

This twofold analysis can help identify best practice companies in each industry sector. A best-in-class manager's aim, therefore, is to invest primarily in companies making the most effort to adhere to ESG criteria, thus prioritising companies displaying exemplary sustainability performance.

Best-in-class is intended to promote positive changes—in other words, to encourage companies to improve their conduct and act more responsibly in order to be attractive for ESG-focused investors. The best-in-class approach is used to create portfolios that give precedence to the most sustainable companies in each sector, leading to diversified portfolios representative of the global economy but slanted towards companies displaying more sustainable practices.

The Different Forms of the Best-in-Class Approach

When selecting securities for their portfolio, best-in-class asset managers first choose criteria that allow them to designate a company as the best in its particular category. They can choose to reward those that have made the greatest effort with respect to their ESG practices or those that have achieved the best results in a particular area by a specified point in time (for example, in social risk management). These decisions often hinge on the asset manager's investment philosophy, with the companies ranked in accordance with fund-specific management objectives, as described next.

Another essential consideration is the question of the investment universe, which will affect how the best-in-class approach is implemented. Being best in the class is one thing, but investors also need to define appropriate peer groups:

- A **best-in-sector**[1] approach allows asset managers to identify the best-performing companies in a given market sector or service and is therefore best suited to sectoral management.

- The **best-in-universe**[2] approach focuses on the initial universe (independent of sector) and only considers the highest-ranked companies. This may mean excluding certain sectors if their ESG contribution is not deemed satisfactory or if they are excluded by the management company from the beginning.

- One speaks of a **best-effort**[3] (securities) or **best-progress**[4] (real estate) approach when the asset manager seeks to include only companies or real estate fund managers that have made the most progress. These approaches also aim to reward positive momentum, helping to ramp up the spread of best ESG practices.

Whichever method is used, the approach remains resolutely positive and targets the most upstanding or promising players in a given investment universe.

The Security Selection Process

In accordance with the criteria provided by institutional investors, managers of best-in-class funds select the companies in their portfolio based on, for example, an ESG assessment grid and an in-house rating system. The analysis must examine the company's overall relations with its stakeholders and carry out an exhaustive review of ESG factors, as illustrated in **Table 4**.

As sustainable investments have become increasingly popular, selection methods have evolved over the years and asset managers can choose from different procedures to perform extra-financial analysis and select companies, namely from the following two options:

- **Outsource** it in full to sustainability rating agencies[5] and other traditional financial data providers.[6]

- **Combine external resources and internal analysis.** To consolidate their security selection process and adapt it to the desired management philosophy, asset managers are increasingly choosing to use data provided by financial data agencies or directly gather them from the companies concerned. These data are then used by internal specialists to perform analyses.

Using these methods, portfolios are created that have differentiating qualities when compared to global investment allocations but are complementary in profile.

An Issuer-Specific Analysis Approach

The above-described criteria are applied within the context of a best-in-class security selection. This approach naturally needs to be adapted for such issuers as governments and public or semi-public bodies due to their radically different nature and purpose.

For an analysis of government bonds, for example, asset managers need to focus on the country in question and where it stands in terms of the

Table 4.   Non-Exhaustive List of ESG Criteria Used to Select Best-in-Class Securities

Environment	Social	Governance
Climate change	Customer satisfaction	Composition of the board of directors
Carbon emissions	Relations with unions	Structure of the audit committee
Biodiversity	Data protection	Enterprise policy
Depletion of natural resources	Relations with civil society	Anti-corruption policy
Energy efficiency	Equal pay	Compensation committee
Waste management	Policy regarding the hiring of disabled people	Lobbying policy
Water/air pollution	Diversity and non-discrimination of minorities	Whistle-blower protection

environment, social protection, education, justice, and health. They also need to ensure that the country complies with international treaties and conventions to protect the environment and human rights.

Pros and Cons of the Best-in-Class Approach

The best-in-class approach requires substantial internal and/or external resources in terms of analysis. This inevitably involves additional costs, which have to be borne by the end investor, ultimately affecting profitability, although such costs currently follow a diminishing trend. The market is currently evolving in this regard, notably through improvements in data management (big data in particular) as well as competition between index providers, ESG rating agencies, and other data providers with respect to the dissemination of extra-financial data. Lastly, with companies increasingly aware of the importance of addressing environmental, social, and governance issues and new regulations requiring them to publish related data and reports, ESG information is becoming easier to access.

Moreover, the best-in-class approach selects companies based on both financial and ESG analysis. Although the ESG aspect has long been a factor for sensitised investors, the rest of the investor community is expected to follow suit. It remains, nonetheless, an approach aimed at improving *all* existing business sectors and thus the economy as a whole. As such, it is capable of generating long-term performances in line with or even above the market.

Conclusion

The main advantage of the best-in-class approach is to facilitate good practice, dialogue, and reflection. It provides for greater cooperation between investors and asset managers with a view to achieving solutions that are in line with both the investment philosophy and the desired return. This considered, it is particularly suited for institutional investors who wish to comprehensively incorporate the theme of social responsibility into their selection to a defined degree, while bringing in their individual view on sustainability.

Further Reading

- Krosinsky, C., Robins, N., & Viederman, S. (2011). *Evolutions in sustainable investing: Strategies, funds and thought leadership*. Hoboken, NJ: John Wiley & Sons.

- Staub-Bisang, M. (2011). *Nachhaltige Anlagen für institutionelle Investoren*. Zürich: Verlag Neue Zürcher Zeitung.

Endnotes

[1]Hancock, J. (2005). *An investor's guide to ethical & socially responsible investment funds*. Kogan Page Publishers.

[2]See previous note for more information.

[3]Eurosif. (2014). *European SRI study 2014*. Available at: http://www.eurosif.org/wp-content/uploads/2014/09/Eurosif-SRI-Study-20142.pdf.

[4]Lambert, A. (2013). *Les fonds immobiliers ISR à la recherche d'une définition standard (SRI Property Funds in Search of a Standard Definition)*. AGEFI. Available in French at: http://www.agefi.fr/articles/les-fonds-immobiliers-isr-a-la-recherche-d-une-definition-standard-1290441.html.

[5]The leading ones in Europe are Inrate, Oekom-GES, Vigeo-Eiris, and Sustainalytics.

[6]Extra-financial data providers, such as Bloomberg, MSCI, and Thompson Reuters, supply ESG data.

Case Study: Eltaver AG

A family office aligns investments with family values.

Information on the organisation	
Type of organisation	Family Office
Assets under management (as of 31.12.2016)	No details
Approximate asset allocation (as of 31.12.2016)	No details
Information on sustainable investment policy	
Who initiated the drafting of a sustainable investment policy?	The female family members in particular showed increased interest in responsible investing. Simultaneously, within the Asset Manager team there was also growing interest in sustainable investments and the family welcomed appropriate proposals.
What was the main motivation for this step?	The main motivation was the family members' wish to align investments with their personal values. In addition, the integration of sustainability criteria fits nicely with the "Value Investing" approach already adopted: the family has a long-term investment horizon. From the asset management perspective, the sustainable investment approach also serves to identify risks at an early stage and supplies ideas for new investment opportunities (attractive sectors, business models, or innovative companies).
What are the main components/content of the sustainable investment policy?	The Family Office invests in various asset classes, but the sustainability integration has so far focused mainly on the equity portfolio. The investment policy is based on a combination of ethical exclusion criteria (gambling, tobacco, weapons, nuclear energy) and a best-in-class approach. The portfolio's carbon intensity is also reviewed periodically.
How was the sustainable investment policy implemented?	Implementation took place in stages. The family has always applied ethical exclusion criteria. Eltaver has been investing in micro-finance since 2008, and the carbon footprint of the share portfolio was measured for the first time in 2011. The various activities highlighted the need to go further and take a more systematic approach towards the integration of sustainability criteria. This led to the additional adoption of the best-in-class approach: Financial instruments are only eligible for investment if they are rated as sustainable. Sustainability criteria are also considered in the quantitative analysis and therefore influence every investment decision.
What resources have been deployed for this?	Eltaver relies on partner banks for defining the sustainable investment universe. The analysis of the portfolio's carbon footprint is based on yourSRI. Sustainability aspects are assessed internally as part of the quantitative analysis. Here, the emphasis is less on the scrutiny of specific indicators and more on a general assessment of risks based on common sense.

What were your experiences with the policy implementation?	Implementation has turned out to be relatively straightforward. Some of the family members and asset managers were convinced by the added value created by sustainability integration, while others were persuaded by the wider benefits. The family gave the asset managers free rein in implementing their ideas under the condition that financial performance was not compromised.
What were notable difficulties?	There were no major difficulties. However, the limited (personnel) resources imply it is not always easy to stay informed on the rapid developments in sustainability themes. So far, however, this has not held back the steady expansion of sustainability integration.
What do you consider to be the main benefits of your sustainable investment policy?	The sustainable investment policy helps to minimise risks as the sustainability rating of a company can be seen as an indicator for good corporate governance. The integration of ESG criteria builds confidence in investment decisions, allowing short-term volatility to be more easily dealt with. It also provides a different perspective and generates new investment ideas. Last but not least, an investment with a positive impact always elicits positive emotions.

9. ESG Integration Approach

Dr. Daniel Wild
Head of Sustainability Investing Research & Development, Member of the Executive Committee, RobecoSAM AG

Sustainability Integration Strategy

With the growth of sustainable investing, a variety of approaches for using sustainability (ESG)[1] data have emerged. The "ESG Integration" strategy in particular has had a lot of traction in recent years. Global Sustainable Investment Alliance[2] states that ESG integration is the second largest sustainable investment strategy globally, with USD10.37 trillion in assets under management (AuM). According to Eurosif,[3] integration is defined as "the explicit inclusion by asset managers of ESG risks and opportunities into traditional financial analysis and investment decisions."

There are different levels on which sustainability information can be integrated into an investment process. This information can be used in the process of identifying an appropriate asset allocation, both on a regional or sector level (see chapter 9.2). More frequently it is used within traditional financial evaluation of issuers for selection of appropriate investments, both on an equity and fixed-income level. Sustainability integration can have a qualitative form when financial analysts cover ESG topics for the in-depth analysis of a company's strengths and weaknesses and take these insights into account in their recommendations (see chapter 9.3). The integration can also have a more quantitative form, when the input factors in a financial model are adjusted based on sustainability information (see chapter 9.1). Although integration approaches have primarily been used in active asset management strategies thus far, the rise of more passive and smart beta strategies over the recent past has seen a corresponding increase in interest in index-based ESG integration approaches.

Just as we observe a variety of investment approaches, we also see a variety of approaches to sustainability integration. This chapter focuses on how sustainability factors can be integrated into a financial model for stock analysis, in the sense of a "systematic inclusion of ESG research in ratings/valuations by analysts and fund managers," as defined in the Eurosif RI Study 2014.[4] This requires not only the consideration of sustainability issues in the investment process but also a demonstration of the impacts that these issues have on the assumptions and the valuation of companies.

Materiality as a Starting Point

Integration into financial models first requires a focused and in-depth understanding of the most material factors that affect a company's business case and, therefore, its financial performance. The most material sustainability factors that inform this analysis can be determined by examining which factors have the greater potential to impact the business value drivers and specifically the assumptions around growth (through future revenue generation), cost (through greater efficiencies), and risk (through the management quality of the company). This analysis of the most material factors must be performed on a sector basis, given that the factors influencing the financial case will be sector-specific. In terms of effectiveness and efficiency, it is reasonable to focus the analysis on the 3–4 sustainability factors that have the biggest impact on the assumptions in the financial model.

The Importance of Time Horizons and Assumptions

In addition to specific material factors, it is important to clarify in which time frame these factors have the most significant impact. Most fundamentally, sustainability factors can have an impact on a company's competitive advantage over longer time frames, either in terms of product differentiation, cost efficiency, or more effective risk management. ESG factors therefore generally play out in terms of the company's financial results over a longer period (more than three years) and thus impact long-term views of company performance. Given the importance of long-term assumptions in most discounted cash flow models, sustainability factors can provide essential information to financial analysts in determining long-term value drivers.

Most financial analysts make projections for the next one to three years based on a company's product mix, competitive positioning, and management guidance. A common approach by analysts to determine the projections in the model after year three is to use assumptions for the future based upon historical averages for the industry across the economic cycle. While such an approach is reasonable and accepted, it does not take into account the company's strategic direction and its unique differentiating qualities that will affect long-term business success. Although the cash flows beyond year three may be difficult to forecast and are increasingly discounted, most of the value of the firm is ultimately derived from these future cash flows in the model (terminal value).

Assessing the long-term positioning and the management quality of a firm can provide essential insights to gain more informed assumptions on future value drivers to be used in the model. Companies that have sales exposure to long-term sustainability trends, such as energy efficiency and reducing climate risks, can be expected to achieve higher long-term sales growth compared to their sector peers. Companies able to demonstrate cost efficiencies through effective environmental management should achieve better margins than the industry average over time. In addition, companies that exhibit outstanding corporate governance or risk management should benefit from lower risk and consequently a lower cost of capital over the long term. Sustainability factors can thus provide important insights that can supplement the shorter-term financial projections that are the focus of most financial analysis, through their integration into longer-term assumptions essential for most financial models.

Integration into Stock Analysis: A Practical Example

The example of a Japanese industrial company that produces electrical equipment and automation products is used to demonstrate the significant impact that sustainability factors can have in a financial model. The analysis of the company's sector, positioning, and financial results leads to basic assumptions based on the company's past performance and reported results. These are used in the model as a starting point, without considering any sustainability factors. The long-term sales growth in the company's end markets is anticipated to be 5%, with an operating margin of 7.5%; a discount rate of future cash flows follows the industry average of 9.0%, which in the discounted cash flow model leads to a target price of JPY3.725 per share (see **Table 5**).

By taking into account the company's sustainability performance, however, the analyst can attain a more informed view of long-term assumptions in the model that better reflects the company's sustainability positioning and competitive advantage. For example, the fact that the company orients its product strategy clearly towards energy efficiency can result in a higher growth rate compared to peers over time. Furthermore, if the company clearly identifies long-term environmental and social trends as a basis for its strategy, this can also result in above-average growth. These factors lead the analyst to an assumed 1.5% higher long-term sales rate relative to sector peers (see Table 5).

In addition to contributing to growth, the company's energy-efficient products tend to offer a higher margin than the rest of the company's portfolio. Consequently, as these products face growing demand, this will lead to an estimated 0.5% higher margin over time. Furthermore, this company demonstrates leadership in how it manages its human capital. It is more advanced than its peers in recognising the importance of diversity issues both in Japan and the rest of the world, and it also shows positive trends in increasing gender diversity and investing in employee development. Given that human capital is

Table 5. Impact of Sustainability Factors on the Fair Value of a Japanese Industrial Company

Value Driver	Sales Growth	Margins	Weighted Average Cost of Capital (WACC)	Fair Value
Benchmark	5% peer average automation	7.5% Operating Margins	9.0%	JPY3.725
Assumptions: ESG adjustment (1): Innovation and Product Stewardship	Positioning on energy efficiency and innovative product range: +150 bps	Product differentiation and competitive positioning: +50 bps		JPY4.050
ESG adjustment (2): Human Capital		Strong human capital performance: +50 bps		JPY4.175
ESG adjustment (3): Governance			Strong corporate governance relative to peers: −50 bps	JPY4.400
Adjusted Assumptions:	**6.5% LT topline growth**	**8.5% Operating Margins**	**8.5%**	**JPY4.400**

a significant expense for the company and expenditures here are important for attracting the right talent, the company's leadership in human capital management leads to lower turnover and higher productivity. The analyst estimates this to have a positive contribution to the company's margin of approximately 0.5% over time compared to the rest of the industry. Combined, these two assumptions lead to a 1% higher estimate than for company margins.

Finally, the company demonstrates leadership in corporate governance, particularly in comparison to its Japanese peers. The company has clear commitments to board diversity and relatively transparent policies. Its independent directors bring relevant experience and strong competencies to the board. The good corporate governance is taken as an indicator for high-quality management, reducing strategic and operational risks. The analyst therefore reduces the weighted average cost of capital (WACC) by approximately 0.5%.

Taking into account the long-term factors that impact the company's performance and explicitly integrating them into a model can be beneficial. Firstly, it is easier to identify the positive contribution that long-term sustainability factors have on the company's fair value in the financial model. In the example, even relatively minor changes in the long-term assumptions coming from sustainability performance lead to a quite significant increase of 18% in the target price (from JPY3.725 to JPY4.400). As illustrated by this example, the integration of sustainability factors can lead to an estimated fair value that lies well above market estimates, therefore underlining the importance of long-term assumptions in the financial model and the significant role that sustainability can play in providing better-informed assumptions. Secondly, systematically integrating sustainability into the financial analysis helps ensure that the portfolio manager can follow a recommendation that integrates both financial and ESG factors consistently and coherently. Although ESG integration may result in a lower than average sustainability performance of a portfolio compared to a purely "best-in-class" approach, it nonetheless has the advantage of allowing the investor to overcome the all-too-frequent trade-off between financial performance on the one hand and sustainability performance on the other. Combining the two perspectives into an integrated financial analysis ensures that portfolio managers receive price signals from the research analyst that include relevant sustainability factors.

This comprehensive example shows how a company's fair value is positively influenced by sustainability factors. When systematically integrated into the research process, sustainability considerations will lead to portfolios with core holdings in companies with a strong sustainability profile that are also likely to outperform over the long term. In other words, if sustainability insights are taken into account, companies with a strong sustainability performance are more likely to be selected for a portfolio than other sector peers. Conversely, the fair value of companies with a poor sustainability performance will be negatively influenced, making the company less attractive for inclusion in investment portfolios (see **Figure 5**).

Figure 5. Typical Sustainability Integration/ESG Integration Approach for Portfolio Selection

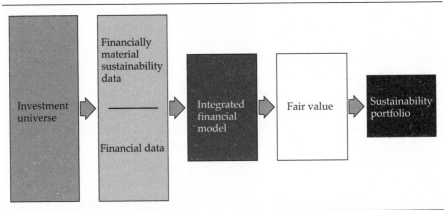

Source: RobecoSAM.

Conclusion

The example used to illustrate integration relates specifically to stock selection. However, a similar approach could be applied to many other levels within the investment process. Through the integration of sustainability factors into financial assumptions, portfolio managers obtain signals that encourage investments in more sustainable regions, sectors, and companies. Such investments are likely to have better long-term growth prospects and reduced risks. A sustainability integration approach can therefore be a means to improve the long-term performance of an actively managed portfolio.

Further Reading

- PRI. (2016). *A practical guide to ESG integration for equity investing.* Available at: https://www.unpri.org/news/pri-launches-esg-integration-guide-for-equity-investors.

- Schramade, W. (2016). Integrating ESG into valuation models and investment decisions: The value-driver adjustment approach. *Journal of Sustainable Finance & Investment*, 6(2), 1–17. Available at: http://www.tandfonline.com/doi/abs/10.1080/20430795.2016.1176425?journalCode =tsfi20.

- Trunow, N.A., & Linder, J. (2015). *Perspectives on ESG integration in equity investing: An opportunity to enhance long-term, risk-adjusted investment performance.* Calvert Investments. Available at: http://www.sustainablefinance.ch/upload/cms/user/201507_Calvert_Perspectives OnESGIntegrationInEquityInvesting.pdf.

- WBCSD & UNEP FI. (2010). *Translating ESG into sustainable business value.* Available at: http://www.unepfi.org/fileadmin/documents/trans-latingESG.pdf.

Endnotes

[1]Sustainability integration is used interchangeably with ESG integration throughout this chapter.
[2]Global Sustainable Investment Alliance. (2016). *Global sustainable investment review 2016.* Available at: http://www.gsi-alliance.org/wp-content/uploads/2017/03/GSIR_Review2016.F.pdf.
[3]Eurosif. (2014). *European SRI study 2014.* Available at: http://www.eurosif.org/sri-study-2014/.
[4]Ibid.

9.1. Enhancing the Investment Process through ESG Integration

Philip Ammann, CFA
Global Thematic Equities Analyst, Vontobel Asset Management

Vontobel mtx has been applying a proprietary framework for ESG assessments since 2010 within one of their asset management teams. This framework is integrated into the investment process for developed and emerging markets with the aim of improving the risk/return profile of investments. The ESG integration approach is characterised by these key points:

- **ESG is a fundamental part of the investment process undertaken by the financial analysts**: The investment process is based on four pillars: above-average return on invested capital (ROIC), strong industry positioning, intrinsic value, and effectively addressing ESG issues. Companies have to fulfil all of the requirements defined within these four pillars in order to qualify for investment.

- **ESG analysis is fully integrated into company evaluations**: The same team of analysts undertakes both ESG and financial evaluations. This enables the analysts to reach decisions based on a holistic understanding of each company. Furthermore, they can adjust their financial models according to risks identified in their ESG evaluations.

- **Development of proprietary Minimum Standard Frameworks**: These sector-specific Minimum Standard Frameworks (MSF) highlight and weigh a broad range of company-specific ESG aspects in a comprehensive ESG evaluation. The financial analysts synthesise their own analysis with the qualitative input from external providers. In addition, they evaluate forward-looking trends, such as ESG initiatives that companies have in the pipeline.

- **Independent ESG audit validates analysis**: When selecting an ESG integration approach, an independent audit is key. An ESG professional, not otherwise involved in the investment process, ensures that the MSF scores are a true reflection of a company's ESG performance. The ESG professional's assessment is not influenced by an otherwise potentially strong investment case.

After several years of following this integration approach, the team wanted to gain a better understanding of the added value of the proprietary ESG assessment methodology. A test was performed to compare companies across all sectors that qualify for investment from both an ROIC and industry positioning perspective but that had differing ESG performances as indicated by their global MSF score. Analysts calculated the stock-price development of a basket of top-quartile MSF companies (equal-weighted) versus the performance of a basket with bottom-quartile MSF companies for the period between December 2012 (launch of the global product) and December 2016 (see **Figure 6**). The results show that companies with high MSF scores (i.e., strong ESG performance) would have outperformed companies with low MSF scores (i.e., weak ESG performance). This theoretical outperformance indicates that the defined Minimum Standard Frameworks provide important additional information about a company and are a significant value-adding factor to the investment process.

The review shows that the structured integration of ESG factors into an investment process can be an effective tool to identify attractive investments and create long-term value for investors.

Figure 6. Testing of Proprietary ESG Integration Approach (global, all sectors)*

*The ESG scores are based on the Vontobel mtx proprietary MSFs. The companies fulfil ROIC and industry positioning requirement (total sample size: 230).
Source: Vontobel mtx (2017).

9.2. Optimised Geographical Asset Allocation Thanks to ESG Integration

Philipp Mettler, CFA
Senior Sustainable Investment Analyst, J. Safra Sarasin

The integration of ESG factors into asset management is steadily growing. Even so, it is not yet possible to claim that "non-financial" aspects are systematically and consistently integrated throughout the entire investment process.[1] While greater attention is being paid to ESG criteria when selecting individual securities—whether equities or bonds—this does not generally appear to be the case when it comes to the geographical allocation of funds. It is precisely here that the integration of ESG components provides an opportunity to make a sustained improvement to a portfolio's risk/return profile.

In general, there are two ways of optimising the geographical allocation with the help of ESG data:

1. The aggregation of relevant ESG company ratings on a country basis

2. The use of top-down sustainability ratings of countries[2]

With the first approach, good company sustainability credentials lead to positive country ratings. The second approach is a top-down country analysis that considers ESG factors and therewith brings valuable aspects for achieving financial outperformance into play. Various studies[3] show that such factors as minimal corruption, stable political governance, and strong innovation certainly have an impact on a country's development over the longer term. This is why ESG country ratings often contain indicators on the overall conditions in a country, such as legal certainty, political governance, population structure, and human capital—factors that are by nature relevant for companies. The historical trend in sustainability is thereby just as relevant as a country's current performance (see **Figure 7**).

The reasons for the positive trends in Eastern Europe and Central Asia, and also in Africa (including the sub-Sahara zone), are partly due to the low baseline but also due to structural advances. By contrast, some countries in Central and South America, as well as in the Middle East, struggle to create a suitable environment for sustainable development. Here it should be remembered that the rate of change in emerging/frontier markets is much higher than in developed markets.

Figure 7.   Sustainability Trend Data over Five Years (indexed)

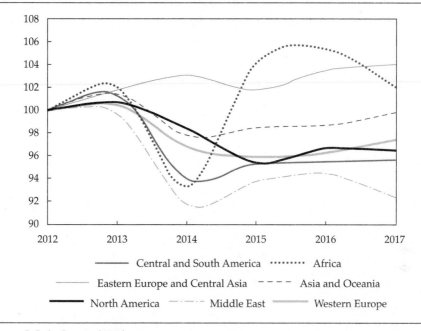

Central and South America · · · · · · · · Africa

Eastern Europe and Central Asia – – – – Asia and Oceania

North America — · — · — Middle East Western Europe

Source: J. Safra Sarasin (2017).

To summarise, ESG country ratings applied to strategic asset allocation can potentially improve a portfolio's risk/return profile. Furthermore, ESG trends can be an indication of structural changes in emerging and frontier markets, especially.

Endnotes

[1]Novethic. (2015). *Profile of responsible investors in Europe.* Available at: http://www.novethic.com/fileadmin/user_upload/tx_ausynovethicetudes/pdf_complets/2015_responsible_investors_survey.pdf.

[2]Primarily to complement credit ratings, where the emphasis is clearly on financial aspects.

[3]Hoepner, A. G., & Neher, A. L. (2013). *Sovereign debt and sustainable development culture.* Available under SSRN 2295688.

9.3. The Role of ESG Integration in Emerging Market Investments

Jürg Vontobel
Founder, Vietnam Holding Asset Management

In most emerging markets, the availability of relevant and reliable environmental, social, and governance (ESG) information remains the key challenge for ESG integration. This is also true for Vietnam, where very few companies report meaningful ESG data. Therefore, it is impossible to gather reliable ESG information through pure desk research. Vietnam currently has the second-highest economic growth rate in Asia, and thus the environmental challenges continue to be immense. Vietnam also has one of the longest coastlines relative to the size of the country. As a result, the climate change challenges, including rising sea levels and saltwater intrusion into the Mekong Delta, continue to loom large.

An Active-Engagement Approach Combined with Public Engagement

VietNam Holding Asset Management (VNHAM) is a value investment manager dedicated to sustainable equity investments in Vietnam. Its flagship fund, VietNam Holding (VNH), signed the UN-supported Principles for Responsible Investment (PRI) in 2009. VNHAM constantly screens the listed company universe in Vietnam by applying a quantitative analytical process based on key value investment and financial parameters. The firms that qualify for an in-depth financial review are simultaneously submitted to an ESG analysis. Visiting analysts submit an elaborate questionnaire based on the methodology of the Swiss ESG research firm Inrate.

In the fund manager's proprietary analytical process, ESG performance is weighted equally with the companies' financial performance. VNHAM reviews its portfolio companies' incremental ESG progress. The openness and willingness of a company to address sustainability challenges proactively is a prerequisite for VNHAM to invest in the companies.

The main challenge is that VNHAM's analysts based in Ho Chi Minh City are mostly in contact with the middle-management levels of the companies. They very seldom have the opportunity to convince the top management of the benefits of sustainability principles, despite increasing publicity of environmental challenges and growing ESG awareness. To overcome this hurdle, the fund manager has developed a direct engagement approach that includes all board members of VNH and VNHAM. Each board member "adopts" several investee companies. The board members are able to engage with the top management of each company at least once a year and seek to obtain very specific commitments to take agreed-upon actions.

The fund manager's disciplined portfolio management is based on three ESG conviction levels:

1. **Limited Conviction:** VNHAM agrees with the portfolio company on the required ESG data to be provided, as well as on specific target parameters to be reached within one year. Until such data are available, the company is classified in this lowest category with a target investment level of 3% of the funds' net asset value (NAV).

2. **Full Conviction:** Once more ESG data are available, and if the company commits to further improving its ESG practices, the company qualifies for category upgrading with a 5% NAV target.

3. **Strong Conviction:** The top-performing companies, both in financial terms as well as in their ESG practices, will qualify for the top status with a 7% NAV target.

The investment process awards portfolio companies' strong financial and ESG performance either with an upgrade or overweighting within the existing conviction range. In the reverse case, the portfolio strategy manager may underweight or downgrade the firm. Each conviction level allows the investment to be adjusted within a defined investment range. On an ongoing basis, VNHAM's analysts spend as much—if not more—time on their portfolio companies' sustainability issues rather than on financial performance. Yet VNHAM feels strongly that it is all worth the effort.

The result of this unique combined approach is commendable: Conservative projections of the VNH portfolio growth show a weighted average EPS growth 2017/2018 of 21.5%—28% higher than the market-consensus EPS growth of 16.8%.[1]

Portfolio Decisions Driven by ESG Analysis

VNHAM has divested from companies more for ESG reasons than for their failings to reach financial performance targets. The most common exit cause was insufficient corporate governance standards. In 2013, Global Witness issued the "Rubber Baron" report on Vietnamese companies' major ESG sins committed through their expansion strategies in Cambodia and Laos.

The very next day, VNHAM initiated an exit from three rubber company investments.

While challenges remain on various fronts, the reporting standards are gradually improving. As of mid-year 2017, 22 out of VNHAM's 28 portfolio companies had sustainability reporting included in their annual report, of which six followed the GRI G4 standard. The other six published a separate high-quality and detailed sustainability report. The willingness to adopt a sustainable strategy reflects a 360° thinking and long-term strategic planning by a company's top management, which in turn results in higher long-term profitability for shareholders. The sustainability journey in Vietnam may still be long, but the consistent progress shows that it can be a very rewarding one.

Endnote

[1]The market-consensus figure was adjusted by excluding three highly speculative companies, which publish ultra-high EPS growth figures in combination with a micro free-float.

Case Study: Zurich Insurance Group

An insurance company broadly integrates sustainability criteria into its investment processes.

Information on the organisation	
Type of organisation	Insurance
Assets under management (as of 31.12.2016)	Around CHF190 billion
Approximate asset allocation (as of 31.12.2016)	**Asset allocation by asset class:** Bonds and other fixed-income securities: 80% Equities: 6% Real estate: 6% Alternative investments: 2% Cash: 4%
Information on sustainable investment policy	
Who initiated the drafting of a sustainable investment policy?	The initiative came from the Chief Investor Officer, who commissioned the development of a Responsible Investment strategy. This was submitted to the Executive Committee and the Board of Directors and approved in the spring of 2012.
What was the main motivation for this step?	The primary motivation was financial: Systematically integrating sustainability into the investment processes can reduce risks and create new investment opportunities. At the same time, however, the aim is to actively contribute to a more sustainable economy in general and the financial industry in particular—in other words, to achieve a positive impact. It is also expected that a sustainable investment approach is welcomed as a positive step by employees and other stakeholders.
What are the main components/content of the sustainable investment policy?	The sustainable investment strategy is based on the following three pillars: • ESG integration • Impact investing • Cooperation with others on the continuous development of sustainability as a theme ESG integration forms the core and covers both internally (1/3) and externally (2/3) managed funds. It is implemented for all asset classes apart from government bonds and hedge funds. For impact investments, the focus currently is on green bonds and private equity with impact. To promote sustainability in the financial services industry, Zurich Group is an active member of such organisations as PRI, Green Bond Principles, Cambridge University's Investment Leaders Group, and the Global Impact Investing Network.

How was the sustainable investment policy implemented?	To implement ESG integration, concrete elements were defined that each investment team must implement independently, with the support of the central Responsible Investment team: 1) Educate and sensitise all employees about sustainability. To this end, an online training module was developed and internal courses were organised. 2) Access to data and analyses: sustainability ratings were integrated into the internal data platform, and portfolio managers receive access to ESG research and data from an external service provider. 3) Integration into the investment process: ESG themes are integrated into investment meetings and risk reporting. 4) Active Ownership: A strategy for the active exercising of voting rights and for active dialogue with companies is currently being implemented. All four elements are also being fully integrated into the selection criteria, contracts, and monitoring of external asset managers.
What resources have been deployed for this?	A two-man Responsible Investment team manages and coordinates the implementation of the sustainable investment strategy. The ESG research is provided by a suitable data provider. For training, employees must not only use internal courses but also the PRI Academy.
What were your experiences with the policy implementation?	The implementation of a sustainable investment strategy is a process that requires a change in the investment culture. This naturally takes a lot of time and it is important for the Responsible Investment team to work closely with those implementing the strategy to provide the necessary support. Thanks to the clear commitment to the sustainability strategy shown by the Executive Committee and the Board of Directors, as well as a very market-based implementation, there was hardly any resistance to the introduction of the policy.
What were notable difficulties?	The implementation of the comprehensive strategy requires the deployment of substantial resources and it takes time for this approach to be applied across all areas. Since all investment teams are individually responsible for implementation, their sense of responsibility needs to be strengthened and they need to be sensitised to the topic: They need to be given suitable training and the right incentives need to be created. Sustainability goals are therefore systematically integrated into individual target agreements. To encourage the right skills, sustainability expertise was also included in job postings.
What do you consider to be the main benefits of your sustainable investment policy?	The strategy is based on the conviction that the integration of sustainability improves the risk/return profile. However, this is almost impossible to prove in quantitative terms because there is no control group in the implementation phase. The integration of sustainability also has a positive impact on the company's reputation. This makes it easier to recruit motivated staff: Many employees are proud of the sustainable approach. And last but not least, the implementation makes a concrete contribution to a more sustainable world.

10. Exercising Voting Rights

Vincent Kaufmann
CEO, Ethos Foundation

For a socially responsible investor, being able to exercise voting rights at annual general meetings is paramount. In Switzerland, voting is now a legal obligation for pension schemes with direct equity investments in Swiss-listed companies. Due to the growth of passive management, institutional investors have become captive shareholders, making it more important than ever that voting rights be systematically and consistently exercised in the long-term interest of all relevant stakeholders. Voting implies fostering good governance and social responsibility, thus enhancing a company's chance of long-term success.

Legal Responsibility and Obligation to Exercise Voting Rights in Switzerland

According to the Swiss Federal Ordinance against Excessive Remuneration with respect to Listed Stock Companies (ORAb),[1] pension schemes subject to the Vested Benefits Act are obliged to vote at the annual general meetings (AGMs) of Swiss-listed stock companies and to disclose information annually on their voting position (ORAb, Articles 22 and 23). When these pension funds hold the shares indirectly in the form of investment funds, voting and disclosure rights must only be exercised if such shares are held in a single investor fund in accordance with Article 7, paragraph 3 of the Swiss Federal Act on Collective Investment Schemes, or as part of discretionary mandates.

For foreign equities owned directly or through mandates, the responsibility for exercising voting rights lies with the final beneficiary and is on a voluntary basis. When companies are domiciled outside Switzerland, investors are not legally obliged to exercise their voting rights.

For collective capital investments in Swiss or international equities, the responsibility to exercise voting rights lies with the fund's management, which can however choose to delegate this responsibility, which should be captured in a transparent manner in the fund contract. Article 34, paragraph 3 of the Ordinance on Collective Investment Schemes (OPCC)[2] clearly states that funds are obliged to "ensure a degree of transparency … such that investors are in a position to comprehend the manner in which such voting rights are exercised." Investors in collective investment schemes therefore have the right to question the fund management company about the exercise of voting rights. Nowadays, a number of investment funds are quite open about how and according to which directives voting rights have been exercised, and some have gone even further by allowing pension schemes to give voting recommendations for the fund's companies in proportion to their investment holdings.

Defining Voting Guidelines

In order to vote systematically and consistently with respect to all securities in a portfolio, institutional investors need to establish a voting policy that addresses the various topics to be put to the shareholders at the AGM. In Switzerland, as in many other countries, the AGM is the company's highest body, approving the annual report, financial statements, dividends, election and discharge of members of the board of directors, changes to the articles of association, capital increases or reductions, and even the choice of auditors. Since the ORAb came into force in Switzerland, shareholders now also vote on the compensation of the board members and executive management.

For voting guidelines to be established, all topics addressed at the AGM need to be examined in accordance with the requirements of national and international codes of good practice. In Switzerland the Code of Practice for Corporate Governance, drawn up by Swiss corporate union economiesuisse,[3] is a good starting point for information on how to prepare such guidelines. It is also useful to draw on other codes from the investor community, such as the "Global Governance Principles" of the International Corporate Governance Network (ICGN), an international investors' organisation with total assets of USD26 trillion.[4] Responsible investors should also consider extra-financial (ESG) criteria in their voting policy. This is done, for example, by voting "No" on the discharge or (re)election of directors to condemn any serious controversies negatively impacting human health or the natural environment. In addition, they can use shareholder resolutions to draw attention to social or environmental issues. Lastly, it is important to update the voting guidelines regularly to take into account changes in legislation and best practice.

Exercising Voting Rights in Practice

Voting positions can only be formulated after the various items on the agenda have been analysed in detail against the voting guidelines. Once the voting positions have been decided, the vote has to be cast. For Swiss companies with registered shares, this means being recorded in the shareholder register. Bearer shares, on the other hand, must be blocked and the blocking and deposit certificates presented to the companies to request the voting card. This procedure is usually performed by the custodian bank, which is in contact with the shareholder register authorities.

If shareholders are unable to attend the AGM in person, they can delegate their votes to another shareholder or instruct the independent representative, who will be present at the meeting, to vote for them. Since the introduction of the ORAb, companies are obliged to provide electronic voting solutions, allowing shareholders to send their voting instructions to the independent representative. For major institutional investors with a global custody account, certain banks allow electronic voting through voting platforms capable of consolidating an investor's overall positions.

Utilizing Proxy Advisors

Three out of four Swiss AGMs are held in April or May.[5] Significant organisation and resources are required to process the information permitting shareholders to cast an informed vote. Because of this, most institutional investors use proxy advisors, who analyse the company's governance structure and annual report as well as the agenda for the AGM and issue voting recommendations. Certain investors use the proxy advisors' findings to form their own opinion, while others systematically delegate their voting rights to these agencies, who are then also responsible for casting the vote.

When it comes to international shares, investors tend to diversify their holdings in different parts of the world, and proxy advisors are therefore often brought in because of the enormous resources that would be required to exercise voting rights for each investment. There is a wide range of these advisors, some of which include environmental and social considerations alongside the traditional corporate governance considerations in their voting recommendations.

If proxy advisors are to have an irreproachable business conduct in the best interests of their clients, it is absolutely vital that they act independently and avoid conflicts of interest, in particular by ensuring that voting guidelines are public, clear, and easy to access. Proxy advisors must also avoid any conflict of interest that could arise, such as if they were to sell consulting services to the companies they analyse. Should such a situation arise, it must be clearly documented in the proxy advisor's analysis.

In cases of doubt and before a "No" vote, it is important that investors contact the company in question and discuss any contentious issues. Recent experience shows that an opposition level of even 10% sends a strong signal to boards of directors, who will then often seek dialogue with critical shareholders (see **Table 6**).

Table 6. 2017 Average Rate of Approval of Board of Directors' Proposals at the AGM (Swiss companies)

	SPI		SMI		SMIM	
	2017	2016	2017	2016	2017	2016
Rate of approval of board of directors' resolutions	95.6%	96.5%	95.3%	96.3%	94.4%	96.2%

Source: Ethos study on the 2016 annual general meetings (2017).

Shareholder Resolutions at Annual General Meetings

The AGM is an excellent opportunity to check if portfolio companies are complying with good practice and with the principles set out in the investor's voting policy. Investors can use the AGM to engage in constructive dialogue with the board of directors and, if this does not pay off, may have to resort to other measures.

Speaking at an AGM is an initial means of putting forward any questions or dissensions to the board of directors. Shareholders can also propose resolutions for inclusion on the AGM's agenda. In Switzerland, the Code of Obligations authorises shareholders holding shares with a value equivalent to CHF1 million (or less if so stated in the articles of association) to add resolutions to the AGM's agenda. In the US, shareholders need only hold shares with a market value of USD2,000 for one year. Although most shareholder resolutions in the US are not binding in nature, it is there that such resolutions are the most common. During the 2017 AGM season, 278 environmental-, social-, or governance-related resolutions were added by shareholders to the agendas of the top 250 companies traded in the United States (see **Figure 8**). Of particular note is the filing by shareholders at Exxon Mobil, Occidental Petroleum Corp, and PPL Corp AGMs of resolutions requesting the boards to assess the risk of tighter climate change-related regulations for the companies. These resolutions were approved by a majority of shareholders despite the boards' opposing recommendations.

In certain recent cases in Europe, the filing of a resolution was even enough to prompt the board to adopt a public stance in favour of a shareholder's proposal. At the 2015 AGMs of BP and Shell, for example, the two companies' boards of directors supported a proposal by a coalition of 150 shareholders requesting an investigation on whether the companies' business was compatible with the goal of limiting global warming to below the two-degree threshold. This proposal was accepted by over 90% of shareholders.

Figure 8.   ESG Resolutions at the AGMs of the Top 250 Companies Traded in the US

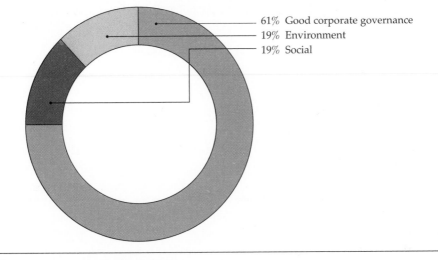

61% Good corporate governance
19% Environment
19% Social

Source: www.proxymonitor.org (2017).

The Importance of Voting

Exercising voting rights is fundamental to the fiduciary duty of all socially responsible, long-term institutional investors, in particular when they manage assets of numerous beneficiaries. This notion of fiduciary duty is described in the "Guidelines for institutional investors governing the exercising of participation rights in public limited companies,"[6] notably in the first principle, which states that "Institutional investors are to exercise their participation rights insofar as this is deemed appropriate and feasible in the interests of their clients."

Exercising voting rights allows investors to approve the activities and direction of the company set by the board of directors or, where necessary, express their disapproval and request improvements in governance and social responsibility. Voting transparency is also an excellent way to initiate constructive dialogue with boards of directors with a view to improve a company's practices. Due to the voting procedure, the AGM remains a listed company's highest body and guarantor of decisions that will influence the creation of long-term value for all relevant stakeholders.

Further Reading

- Bundesrat. (2014). *Verordnung gegen übermässige Vergütung bei börsenkotierten Aktiengesellschaften*. Available in German at: https://www.admin.ch/opc/de/classified-compilation/20132519/index.html.

- Economiesuisse. (2016). *Swiss code of best practice for corporate governance.* Available at: http://www.economiesuisse.ch/sites/default/files/publications/economiesuisse_swisscode_e_web_0.pdf.

- International Corporate Governance Network (ICGN). (2016). *Policy.* Available at: https://www.icgn.org/policy.

- Responsible Investor. (2016). *ESG magazine: Investors move to governance checkmate.* Issue 04. Available at: http://www.esg-magazine.com/.

Endnotes

[1]Swiss Federal Council. (2014).

[2]Swiss Federal Council. (2015). Available at: https://www.admin.ch/opc/en/classified-compilation/20062920/201501010000/951.311.pdf.

[3]economiesuisse. (2016). *Swiss Code of Best Practice for Corporate Governance.* Available at: http://www.economiesuisse.ch/de/publikationen/swiss-code-best-practice-corporate-governance-english-0.

[4]International Corporate Governance Network. (2016). *Policy.* Available at: https://www.icgn.org/policy.

[5]Ethos study on 2015 annual general meetings, compensation and governance in SPI companies. Available in German at: http://www.ethosfund.ch/sites/default/files/upload/publication/p591d_151001_Ethos_Studie_ber_die_Schweizer_Generalversammlungen_.pdf.

[6]economiesuisse. (2013). *Guidelines for institutional investors governing the exercising of participation rights in public limited companies.* Available at: http://www.ethosfund.ch/sites/default/files/upload/publication/p432e_130121_Guidelines_for_institutional_investors.pdf.

Case Study: Pension Fund of the City of Zurich

A public pension fund also gets involved as an active shareholder in foreign companies.

Information on the organisation	
Type of organisation	Public sector pension fund
Assets under management (as of 31.12.2016)	CHF16.02 billion
Approximate asset allocation (as of 31.12.2016)	**Asset allocation by asset class:** CHF bonds: 9% Foreign currency bonds: 14% Swiss equities: 7% Global equities: 33% Real estate (incl. mortgages): 15% Others: 23% **Asset allocation by region:** Switzerland: 31% Global: 69%
Information on sustainable investment policy	
Who initiated the drafting of a sustainable investment policy?	The initiative originally came from the Board of Trustees' Investment Committee, which focused on the pension fund's role as a shareholder at a meeting in 2003 and invited Ethos to a workshop. A decision was then made in 2004 to actively exercise voting rights for Swiss companies and to co-found the Ethos Engagement Pool.
What was the main motivation for this step?	The "principal/agent" issue was the key trigger for this discussion. The Investment Committee was of the opinion that company management does not automatically operate in the interests of shareholders, and that shareholders must play an active role in ensuring the adequate representation of their interests. In the initial phase, the focus was mainly on the criteria of good corporate governance, but equal importance is now given to environmental and social themes.

What are the main components/content of the sustainable investment policy?	The purpose of the sustainable investment policy is to contribute to a sustainable economy that is successful in the long run, thereby securing long-term investment opportunities. The main instrument is an active dialogue with companies to encourage them to adopt more sustainable business practices. On top of that, the voting rights for Swiss companies, as well as 300 other large global companies, are actively exercised. Serious violation of economic, social, or environmental standards, as defined in the Global Compact, leads to an exclusion of the company from investment, unless an improvement can be achieved through open dialogue. Manufacturers of controversial weapons are also excluded. In the summer of 2016, around 30 companies were on the exclusion list, which is published online. The exclusions also apply to bonds issued by the companies in question.
How was the sustainable investment policy implemented?	The elements of the sustainability strategy were integrated into the investment policy and the investment regulations. The PKZH relies on specialist consultants both for exercising voting rights and for active dialogue with companies. The exclusion policy was integrated into the agreements with external asset managers. For passive investments, customised indices for the PKZH are used that omit the excluded companies altogether.
What resources have been deployed for this?	To implement and support the sustainability strategy, we allot 20% of an FTE (full-time employee). Since 2004 the PKZH has been working with Ethos for recommendations on the exercising of its voting rights for Swiss companies. In the same year, the PKZH and a Geneva Pension Fund co-founded the Ethos Engagement Pool. In 2011, Hermes EOS was chosen as a partner for engagement and exercising of voting rights in foreign companies. PKZH maintains an exclusion list using the information supplied by Hermes EOS.
What were your experiences with the policy implementation?	Exercising voting rights can be more difficult in some countries than in Switzerland and can also be very expensive. Dialogue themes can be agreed upon in consultation with the advisors and their customers. Although the dialogue usually produces positive results, it can sometimes take longer than desired. The implementation costs are acceptable due to the large volume.
What were notable difficulties?	It was not easy to apply the exclusion policy to passive investments. But since these make up a large portion of the portfolio, our solution was to commission the creation of a customised index, omitting the excluded companies.
What do you consider to be the main benefits of your sustainable investment policy?	The exercising of voting rights and company dialogue can be applied—independently of individual investment vehicles and mandates—to companies and subsequently to the associated equity and bond securities in the sense of a policy overlay. The process is clear and easy to communicate. The exclusions have resulted in a slightly different sector weighting, which has, in turn, had a slightly positive impact on performance in the past years.

11. Shareholder Engagement—Dialogue with Companies

Andrea Gäumann
Consultant, BHP—Brugger and Partners Ltd.

Regula Simsa, CFA
Consultant, BHP—Brugger and Partners Ltd.

In addition to established SRI strategies—such as the application of exclusion criteria, best-in-class approaches, or the extensive integration of ESG factors into financial analysis (see chapters 7, 8, and 9)—shareholder engagement is becoming an increasingly important approach for institutional investors. Shareholder engagement not only includes the exercising of voting rights (see chapter 10) but also the active interaction of shareholders with portfolio companies regarding ESG themes. As legitimate stakeholders, shareholders are entitled to protect their own interests. According to the definition provided by Eurosif,[1] engagement is part of a long-term process in which shareholders attempt to influence a company's business conduct. This is done in order to improve governance, give greater consideration to environmental and social aspects, or encourage more transparent information—thereby improving the company's ability to deal with long-term challenges. The central aspect is dialogue between the management of the portfolio company and investors (or their representatives). This approach is based on the assumption that engagement helps increase enterprise value, since ESG criteria also have an impact on value creation and allow such other factors as reputation risks to be controlled more effectively. Besides influencing business practices through engagement, the focus may also be to obtain additional information. Through their dialogue with companies, portfolio managers obtain insights that enable them to understand or assess the business models more effectively.

Shareholder Engagement: Background and Development

Engagement as part of active equity ownership is based on the classical principal/agent theory. Institutional asset managers, such as pension funds or fund managers, must ensure that the board and management of investee companies act in the best interests of the shareholders they represent.

According to the second principle of the UN-supported Principles for Responsible Investment (PRI),[2] responsible investors make the following commitment: "We will be active owners and incorporate ESG issues into ownership policies and practices." Possible actions to achieve this commitment include "develop an engagement capability" and "engage with companies on ESG issues" and also "ask investment managers to undertake and report on ESG-related engagement."

In many respects, engagement offers investors the opportunity to create added value (see Eurosif, 2013):

- Development of business strategy better equipped to deal with long-term challenges

- Reduction of reputational risks

- Maximisation of risk-adjusted returns

- Contribution towards sustainable development

- Improvement of ethical business conduct

- Fulfilling fiduciary duties

- Improvement of information base available on portfolio companies

Shareholder engagement has steadily increased over the last 10 years (see **Figure 9**).

The increase in shareholder engagement also reflects regulatory trends. In more and more European markets, voluntary codes of commitment have been introduced for asset managers where the signatories must pledge to carry out

Figure 9. Increase in Engagement and Exercising of Voting Rights in Europe

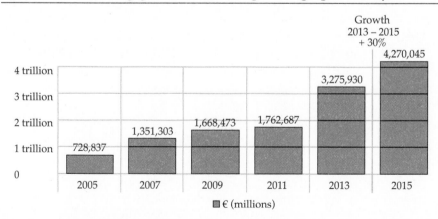

Source: Eurosif European SRI Study (2016).

engagement activities.[3] Suitable guidelines are currently being prepared at the EU level. These will require asset owners to meet their fiduciary obligations to counter the trend towards "rudderless" companies.

Phases of the Engagement Approach

Ideally, an engagement approach passes through different phases (see **Figure 10**). In the initial definition phase, the engagement guideline, objectives, and topics of engagement are determined. In the second phase, portfolio companies are analysed and their potential and risks identified. Next, in the third phase, a dialogue with the company's representatives is initiated in which existing shortcomings and potential measures for improvement are discussed. In the fourth step, the results from the interaction are reported to investors and any agreements on targets and recommended actions are formulated, which are, in turn, reviewed in another cycle of engagement. This is therefore a multi-stage, iterative process based on the principle of continuous improvement, which requires a structured approach. If, despite the proactive engagement, there seem to be no changes in a "critical" portfolio company, additional steps need to be considered. Potential measures range from deepened discussions with individual representatives from the management or the board, to the submission of proposals to the annual general meeting, to even divestment as a last resort. It needs to be emphasised that after a divestment no further shareholder engagement is possible and that a company can no longer be directly influenced.

Forms of Shareholder Engagement

In contrast to such SRI approaches as best-in-class or the application of exclusion criteria, an engagement approach is only initiated if companies are already included in the portfolio. The purpose of engagement is to encourage systematic integration of relevant ESG aspects into the corporate strategy and the core business by making concrete recommendations and exerting influence. Another goal is to allow information from the engagement to flow into the investment decision to improve and reinforce the portfolio managers' basis for making decisions. While the first approach focuses on the impact

Figure 10.   Engagement Phases

on the company (exerting influence), in the second approach, engagement is also used as a way of optimising portfolio management (obtaining information and using it in the investment process).

The second approach brings direct benefit for fund managers in their future work but assumes ESG know-how is available, as well as the willingness to invest time in engagement.

Furthermore, approaches also differ depending on whether an institutional investor is striving for a direct dialogue with the portfolio companies or if the engagement is part of a collaboration with other investors. One example of a collaborative approach is the PRI Collaboration Platform,[4] a PRI global platform for collective engagement initiatives. The platform is meant to induce collaboration between several investors, rather than delegating the engagement to independent specialists. Such cooperations offer several advantages: The investor community can access a broader knowledge base, sources are bundled, costs are shared, and negotiating powers are strengthened due to larger shareholdings.

If asset managers do not have the necessary resources for effectively targeted engagement, this task can also be delegated to specialised providers. Due to their specialisation, they often handle different engagements from several investors and, in most cases, can proceed very efficiently. Ideally, portfolio managers are actively involved in the engagement to ensure the learning process and knowledge exchange. There are also combined approaches where sustainability specialists take part alongside fund managers in the dialogue with companies.[5]

Ultimately, the difference between the approaches depends on whether the dialogue is conducted privately behind closed doors or whether the intention is to exert public pressure. From the asset owners' perspective, a more confrontational approach (e.g., the threat of negative publicity or the publication of a list of excluded companies) may be more effective. In this case, however, it could cause the company to terminate the dialogue or only engage to protect its image. If the approach is more cooperative, the dialogue is likely to be more long-term and constructive in character and one built on trust, offering portfolio managers valuable insights into the business.

Impact

Investors measure the impact of their ESG engagements using both qualitative (e.g., number of measures implemented by the companies) and quantitative approaches (e.g., change in ESG ratings). Various meta-studies on financial performance show that engagement can have a measurable impact on performance. A recent study (Dimson et al., 2012) reports that shares of

Figure 11. Cumulative Monthly Abnormal Returns Relative to First ESG Engagement

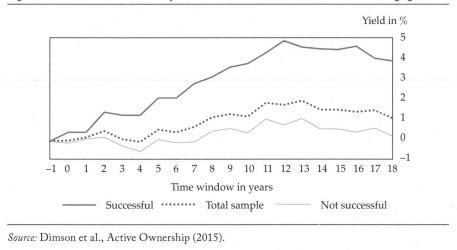

Source: Dimson et al., Active Ownership (2015).

a group of more than 600 "engaged" US corporations were able to achieve a 1.8% improvement in their factor-adjusted performance compared with the overall market just 18 months after the engagement started. In the case of successful engagement (i.e., when recommendations were implemented), this performance was even 4.4% higher, while companies that did not implement the recommendations failed to show any demonstrable impact (see **Figure 11**).[6]

Conclusion

"Active" shareholder engagement requires more resources than the simple exercising of voting rights. However, the extra effort usually pays off: In addition to directly influencing the governance structures and contributing to environmental and social themes, engagement also builds a better information base for making investment decisions. Business practices, management activities, and potential risks of the portfolio companies can be assessed more accurately, thus allowing capital to be allocated more effectively. From the different types of engagement, institutional investors can choose the one that best fits their particular needs: They can delegate this resource-intensive process to external providers or focus their own engagement on selected companies that they believe offer the highest potential impact.[7]

Companies that encourage dialogue with their investors as part of stakeholder engagement receive direct input—often at an early stage—on the expectations, concerns, and priorities of their investors. "Engagers" usually think long-term and have an entrepreneurial mindset. Portfolio companies that do not pay sufficient attention to certain ESG criteria can be influenced more readily by a continuous, focused engagement than if investors were to simply sell the shares in question. Active shareholders can, therefore, not only achieve more competitive returns but also make a significant contribution to changing companies' awareness of ESG factors.

Further Reading

- Carbon Disclosure Project. (2016). *Homepage*. Available at: www.cdp.net.

- Dimson, E., Karakaş, O., & Li, X. (2015). Active ownership. *Review of Financial Studies, 28*(12), 3225–3268. Available at: http://www.people.hbs.edu/kramanna/HBS_JAE_Conference/Dimson_Karakas_Li.pdf.

- Eurosif. (2014). *European SRI study 2014*. Available at: http://www.eurosif.org/wp-content/uploads/2014/09/Eurosif-SRI-Study-20142.pdf.

- Eurosif. (2013). *Shareholder stewardship: European ESG engagement practices 2013*. Available at: http://www.eurosif.org/wp-content/uploads/2014/06/eurosif-report-shareholder-stewardship.pdf.

- Hoepner, A. G., Oikonomou, I., & Zhou, X. Y. (2015). *Private ESG shareholder engagement and risk: Clinical study of the extractive industry*. Available at: SSRN 2681375.

- PRI. (2016). *Collaboration platform*. Available at: https://www.unpri.org/about/pri-teams/esg-engagements/collaboration-platform.

Endnotes

[1] Eurosif. Shareholder stewardship: European ESG engagement practice 2013.

[2] UNPRI. (2016). *The six principles*. Available at: www.unpri.org/about-pri/the-six-principles.

[3] For example, the Financial Reporting Council. (2012). *UK Stewardship Code*: www.frc.org.uk/Our-Work/Codes-Standards/Corporate-governance/UK-Stewardship-Code.aspx.

[4] PRI. (2016). *Collaboration platform*. Available at: www.unpri.org/about/pri-teams/esg-engagements/collaboration-platform.

[5] A good example: the Cadmos Engagement Funds. Available at: https://www.ppt.ch/en/cadmos/.

[6] A more recent study [Hoepner, A.G., Oikonomou, I., & Zhou, X.Y. (2015). *Private ESG shareholder engagement and risk: Clinical study of the extractive industry*. Available at: SSRN 2681375] shows that engagement reduces the downside risks. The CalPERS effect has also been already proven in several studies: After engagement, the companies in question produced significantly higher returns than the overall market.

[7] See CalPERS approach with focus lists.

Case Study: PUBLICA Federal Pension Fund

The Pension Fund of the Swiss Confederation PUBLICA joins forces with other public sector investors for engagement and exclusion.

Information on the organisation			
Type of organisation	Pension fund		
Assets under management (as of 31.12.2016)	CHF37.8 billion (open and closed benefit schemes)		
Approximate asset allocation (as of 31.12.2016)		Open Benefit Schemes	Closed Benefit Schemes
	CHF bonds	18%	41%
	Foreign currency bonds	41%	24%
	Swiss equities	3%	3%
	Global equities	27%	7%
	Real estate	6%	21%
	Others	5%	4%
Information on sustainable investment policy			
Who initiated the drafting of a sustainable investment policy?	The initiative came from the Asset Management team, which had already been tracking the topic for a considerable time. In 2014, the Investment Committee and subsequently PUBLICA's Fund Commission discussed a holistic concept for "responsible investing" in detail.		
What was the main motivation for this step?	Generally speaking, a sustainable investment policy is seen as part of a comprehensive risk management strategy designed to reduce financial risks. As a public sector pension fund, PUBLICA is also more exposed to public attention than other pension schemes, which was an extra incentive to develop the theme further and communicate it in a transparent manner. On top of that, there were occasional enquiries from beneficiaries about the sustainability policy. Even though PUBLICA had been actively exercising voting rights for Swiss shares for some years, holding dialogues with critical companies of concern and excluding individual firms, there was no well-documented foundation for responding to such customer queries. Exchanges with international peers underscored the assumption that the topic would become more important in the future. In addition, PUBLICA was seeking a suitable platform to also hold effective dialogues with foreign companies.		

What are the main components/content of the sustainable investment policy?	The most important requirement for the sustainable investment policy was for it to be built on the basic pillars of the existing investment policy, which focuses on passive investments. The foundation of the sustainability analysis is based on existing environmental, social, and governance (ESG) standards reflected in applicable Swiss law and international agreements. PUBLICA commences a dialogue with companies in clear violation of the respective norms, with the aim to improve the situation. As a "last resort," companies are put on an exclusion list and divested from the portfolio. In parallel, an ESG risk analysis process was introduced that facilitates the assessment of difficult to quantify risks.
How was the sustainable investment policy implemented?	In order to implement this investment policy as effectively as possible, PUBLICA has joined forces with six other large institutional Swiss investors to form the Swiss Association for Responsible Investments (*Schweizer Verein für verantwortungsbewusste Kapitalanlagen, SVVK-ASIR*). This makes it more economical for all members to access the sustainability ratings of equity investments, engage in a dialogue with companies, and make recommendations for exclusions. It is left to individual organisations to implement more far-reaching sustainability strategies. PUBLICA publishes details of its own sustainability policy on its website.
What resources have been deployed for this?	The development of the sustainable investment policy and the foundation of SVVK-ASIR were carried out with internal resources of participating members. In performing its activities, however, the Association works with external partners that provide research capacities and enter into a dialogue with companies on behalf of the Association.
What were your experiences with the policy implementation?	It took very little to persuade the Investment Committee to approve the concept as it aligns with PUBLICA's own investment credo. Important partners signed up in a brief period of time for the SVVK-ASIR's foundation, which only took just over a year. The collective sustainable investment policy is based on the "smallest common denominator." Individual institutions then apply more far-reaching measures. It remains to be seen how consistently the individual members subsequently implement the jointly compiled exclusion list.
What were notable difficulties?	Recently, pension funds have had to deal with many urgent and important issues, such as the financial crisis, the Swiss franc shock, and new regulatory requirements. Therefore, the parties responsible had limited capacity to simultaneously address sustainable investment themes during this period. Setting up the new Association at an affordable cost was another major challenge. Last but not least, there were also discussions on transparency: How frequently should engagement and exclusion be communicated? An initial exclusion list was published on the Association's website in the beginning of March 2017.

What are the main benefits of addressing your sustainable investment policy as part of an Association?	The exclusion of companies in breach of relevant sustainability norms along with additional engagement in the interests of insured members and pensioners strengthens the profile of PUBLICA and other involved investors. Combining forces with other players makes it possible to exercise shareholder rights more effectively abroad, since SVVK-ASIR carries more weight than an individual investor in the dialogue with companies. At the same time, associative collaboration reduces the costs of research activities. Decisions can also be communicated more effectively if made in conjunction with other like-minded parties.

11.1. Shareholder Engagement: Experiences of a Swiss Investor Collective

Vincent Kaufmann
CEO, Ethos Foundation

The Ethos Engagement Pool (EEP) was set up in 2004 by Ethos and two public pension funds convinced that engaging in dialogue with companies is an effective way of raising awareness about sound corporate governance and sustainable business practices. By combining the strengths of several institutional investors that have a shared interest in promoting environmental, social, and corporate governance (ESG) issues, the Pool aims to increase companies' long-term value for all stakeholders. By 31 July 2017, the Ethos Engagement Pool had 133 members representing approximately CHF191 billion assets under management. Engagement topics are chosen annually by the Pool members and revolve around ESG-related matters.

Engagement in Practice

The Ethos Foundation is responsible for the engagement, which can either be with selected companies regarding all relevant subjects or with all of the companies regarding one specific theme. The engagement can be carried out through letters, conference calls, or meetings. Furthermore, the EEP supports the publication of ESG-related studies that enable the comparison of practices in various companies and promotion of best practices with regard to various engagement topics.

Promoting Sustainability-Related Performance

The EEP seeks to promote constructive dialogue between investors and companies to improve their sustainability-related performance. Whilst engagement between shareholders and companies traditionally focused on financial strategy, the EEP was founded to enable Swiss institutional investors to broaden the discussion topics with listed Swiss companies. It works alongside other players in the field of shareholder engagement (see chapter 10) to improve the performance of Swiss companies with regard to:

- Say-on-Pay: Before the approval of the Minder Initiative[1] by the Swiss public, the EEP managed to convince 50 companies to organise an advisory vote on their executive remuneration policies.

- Code of Conduct: the EEP encourages companies to establish a publicaly available code of conduct. When dialogue began about this issue in 2006, only 33% of the 50 companies on the SMI Expanded Index had made their code public. By late 2016, 94% of companies had done so.

- Participation in the Carbon Disclosure Project (CDP)[2]: The EEP actively encourages the voluntary participation of Swiss companies in the CDP. Between 2006 and 2012, when the EEP was responsible for the administration of the Swiss survey, the number of companies taking part increased threefold to 65% of the 100 largest listed Swiss companies, resulting in one of the highest participation levels in the world.

The sheer number of pension funds joining the EEP illustrates that corporate responsibility and good governance are important issues for institutional investors. Joining forces gives these investors significant leverage when holding dialogues with companies about sustainability, thus creating value for all relevant stakeholders.

Endnotes

[1] In 2014, VegüV (Verordnung gegen übermässige Vergütungen bei börsenkotierten Aktiengesellschaften), generally known as the Minder Initiative, came into force. Under this new law, shareholders received more rights in determining the management's remuneration.
[2] Carbon Disclosure Project: an initiative encouraging companies and cities to disclose information about their environmental impact.

Case Study: CAP Prévoyance

A public pension fund aligns its investments with long-term sustainability criteria.

Information on the organisation	
Type of organisation	Public pension fund. Occupational pension fund for the City of Geneva, SIG (Geneva's industrial service provider), 41 Geneva municipalities, six external institutions, and CAP Prévoyance.
Assets under management (as of 31.12.2016)	CHF4.1 billion
Approximate asset allocation (as of 31.12.2016)	**Allocation by asset class** CHF bonds: 5.7% Foreign currency bonds: 13% Swiss equities: 15.7% International equities: 20.3% Real estate: 33% Other: 12.3%
Information on sustainable investment policy	
Who initiated the drafting of a sustainable investment policy?	CAP Prévoyance ("Caisse d'assurance du personnel de la Ville et des Services Industriels de Genève" until late 2013) has been active in sustainable investment since 2001. Both the foundation's Board of Trustees and the executive management support and carry forward the issue.
What was the main motivation for this step?	The approach was mainly driven by the Board of Trustees, which felt that especially a public pension fund should be concerned about and evaluating issues of good corporate governance and sustainable development. In line with the values and principles set out by the City of Geneva, the Board and executive management expressed their intention to invest responsibly so as to finance a sustainable economy. Another reason was long-term vision. Board members are convinced that the incorporation of environmental, social, and corporate governance (ESG) factors is likely to increase the value of the capital on a risk-adjusted return basis.
What are the main components/content of the sustainable investment policy?	Broadly speaking, the 2010 adopted Responsible Investment Charter recommends: • incorporating ESG issues into the management of movable and immovable assets, • exercising voting rights and shareholder dialogue, • excluding companies involved in arms and pornography, and • that CAP does not invest in commodities and hedge funds.

How was the sustainable investment policy implemented?	As early as 2001, CAP Prévoyance decided to exercise its shareholders' rights as extensively as possible and became a member of the Ethos Foundation. It strengthened this commitment in 2009 by joining the Ethos Engagement Pool, whilst at the same time gradually increasing its investments in Swiss and international sustainable equity funds.
	In 2010, the Responsible Investment Charter was drawn up and is now an integral part of the fund's investment regulations and an important milestone in the formalisation of its commitment (www.cap-prevoyance.ch/la-fondation).
	This Charter must be enforced as part of a sound and rigorous financial framework, aiming to meet the financial interests (i.e., profitability of its investments) of CAP Prévoyance, in the long run. The content of the Charter was communicated to all external asset managers and presents responsible investment as a philosophy that can be applied to all assets. Expected returns are similar to those of traditional investments.
What resources have been deployed for this?	The internal team is sensitive and open to issues of long-term sustainable development. To ensure that these issues are included in the investment process, CAP Prévoyance has decided to join the Ethos Engagement Pool and to work regularly with external advisors. It also relies on the asset managers to adjust their investment processes and provide innovative solutions that are compatible with the Charter.
What were your experiences with the policy implementation?	The approach has been well received by partners. This even includes the asset managers whose management solutions were not compatible with the Charter. As CAP Prévoyance is aware that applying the Charter to different asset classes (stocks, bonds, etc.) can lead to additional constraints and risks, it takes a pragmatic approach by applying the principles gradually and prudently. Recent results (2015) are considered sound with regards to developments in the financial markets and reference indices.
What were notable difficulties?	The main impediment is still the current economic, financial, and regulatory environment, which poses numerous challenges that need to be addressed by pension funds if they are to ensure the longevity of their services.
What do you consider to be the main benefits of your sustainable investment policy?	The major benefits are improved transparency and enhanced dialogue with external partners and companies as well as better risk management (for example, controversy monitoring).

This case study was produced with the support of Angela de Wolff, Founding Partner of Conser Invest.

12. Sustainable Thematic Investments

Dr. Marc-Olivier Buffle
Senior Client Portfolio Manager, Pictet

Thematic investing is an investment approach that focuses on specific economic activities that are identified because of their potential for sustaining superior long-term growth.[1] When these activities are of a sustainable nature, the theme can be characterised as sustainable and the approach as sustainable thematic investing.

For a company to qualify as a sustainable thematic investment candidate, it must possess two qualities.

First, a sustainable company should "do the right thing." Its core business should focus on the development of products and services that directly seek to alleviate the strains on the world's natural resources or help overcome societal challenges. It is this quality in particular that can be accessed through sustainable investment themes with specific environmental or societal focus.

Second, a sustainable company should "do things right." In other words, it should actively seek to improve its environmental and societal impact across its operations and beyond—from the way it sources raw materials to how it recycles its products once they become obsolete.

What Is Meant by Thematic Investing

By focusing on themes, asset managers aim to identify segments of the economy that display superior long-term growth. One approach to identify themes is by analysis of secular trends. Long-term changes affecting society and the environment are determined, and those segments of the economy that benefit from such changes are identified. This then leads to the discovery of groups of companies that should experience long-term growth superior to that of the global economy.

Thematic investing is a long-term investment approach: economic cycles might affect returns in the short term, but thematic investors should experience returns superior to those of the market over periods spanning multiple cycles.

As an example, companies developing water-related products and services are supported by the secular trends of urbanisation, growth of the middle class in emerging markets, aging infrastructure in developed markets, climate-change-induced water scarcity, ubiquitous water pollution, and an increasingly global focus on health. Hence, companies that market solutions to meet those challenges should represent attractive investment opportunities. A diversified portfolio taking such an investment universe as a starting point, and constructed using a systematic and fundamental investment process, should lead to superior long-term investment returns, such as the water strategy shown in **Figure 12**, covering a period of 16 years.

Another three sustainable thematic strategies—security, health, and clean energy—are shown in Figure 12. Security demonstrates returns superior to the global equity markets (MSCI) but with lower volatility. Health shows superior returns and higher volatility, while Clean Energy shows greater volatility but lower returns versus the global equity market since inception.

Figure 12. Risk–Return Profile of Sustainable Thematic Strategies (Water, Security, Health, Clean Energy)

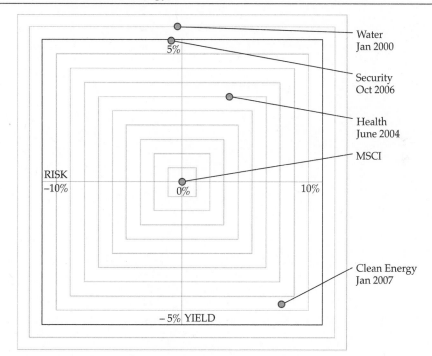

Notes: In USD, since inception, annualised, relative to MSCI, gross of fees. Based on thematic funds of Pictet Asset Management.
Source: Pictet Asset Management (2016).

Characteristics of Thematic Strategies

There are many thematic strategies with diverse investment processes and associated financial characteristics. What follows are examples of some of the most important and distinctive features of thematic investing.[2]

Global and benchmark-agnostic investing. Thematic strategies are typically characterised by investment universes of 200–400 stocks. The only selection criterion for eligibility in the investment universe is the company's theme-related products and services. Hence, the regional and size distributions of thematic investment universes are broader than those of mainstream global indices (e.g., MSCI World excludes emerging and frontier markets as well as micro and small capitalisations, while thematic portfolios typically include them). Additionally, the portfolio construction process is benchmark-agnostic,[3] so that portfolios often display size, regional, and sector biases versus common market-cap-weighted global indices (see **Figure 13**).

Strong focus. Companies become interesting thematic investment candidates only if their field of activity is focused and related to the theme. Unlike

Figure 13. Exposure of a Strategy Invested in Nine Thematic Portfolios Relative to MSCI World

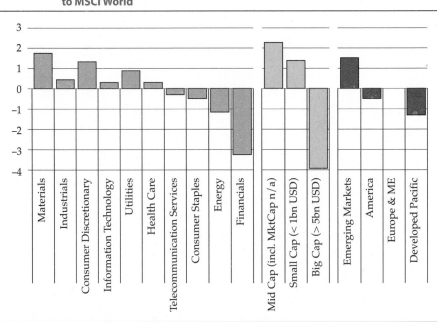

Note: The aggregated relative exposure displayed is often observed in thematic portfolios: no sector neutrality, small- and mid-cap exposure, emerging- and frontier-market exposure.

large conglomerates, they are specialised firms. The degree of exposure to the theme (degree of focus) is a key criterion for the eligibility of a company in a thematic universe. Similarly, a thematic portfolio manager is a specialist with substantial expertise in the investment theme, its segments and drivers. Thematic investment teams know their focused investment universes inside out and often include individuals with technical expertise who have worked in firms that are active within the theme.

Diversifying investment. A consequence of the focus of investment themes and of a truly global and benchmark-agnostic portfolio construction process is that theme-driven portfolios display smaller overlap and higher active share versus common market-cap-weighted global indices compared with traditional global equity portfolios. These characteristics provide diversification within a global equity allocation.

Applying Thematic Investing within an Institutional Context

Even if thematically oriented stocks offer a potentially distinct source of return, pension schemes and insurance companies have traditionally found it difficult to determine how such investments might fit into their portfolios. The discovery of a new portfolio building block often has implications for a scheme's entire asset allocation process—and there are few investors who relish the prospect of carrying out a root-and-branch overhaul of their investment frameworks.

Nevertheless, institutional investors are beginning to find ways to overcome the constraints of traditional asset allocation. A recent survey of global pension schemes, insurers, and sovereign wealth funds by the management consultancy firm McKinsey & Company found that institutional investors are using a variety of approaches to incorporate thematic investments into their portfolios (see **Table 7**). These range from the creation of single- or multi-asset class thematic mandates to the development of thematic views within an existing structure.

How Sustainable Are Sustainable Thematic Strategies?

A theme deemed sustainable ("doing the right thing") does not necessarily imply that its associated business practices are sustainable ("doing things right").

There is no global standard for the investment process adopted to construct sustainable theme portfolios. Different asset managers might include

Table 7.   Range of Approaches to Develop Thematic-Investing Strategies

Lower commitment to thematic strategy → Higher commitment to thematic strategy

	Lower commitment to thematic strategy			Higher commitment to thematic strategy
APPROACH	Develop thematic views within the existing structure. Develop and implement thematic investments within the risk limits and structure of the current portfolio	Construct a thematic overlay. From the centre, establish a thematic overlay portfolio or shift asset allocations and increase their duration based on house views on sector/geography	Create a single-asset-class thematic mandate. Allocate capital to portfolios or mandates with investment strategies that rely on developing forward-looking thematic views	Create a multi-asset-class thematic mandate. Create a thematic fund to generate the most attractive long-term risk-adjusted returns by investing in various asset classes
EXAMPLE	Use current risk limits in an international equity portfolio to increase exposure-specific solar-module producers in response to a renewable energy theme	Gain long-term exposure to wheat price by investing in wheat futures as part of a thematic overlay portfolio	Create and capitalise an equity portfolio with a clear purpose of gaining long-term exposure to renewable energy	Create a portfolio – governed by a multi-asset-class committee – looking into technology investments through a combination of venture capital funds, direct private-equity investments, and public-equity positions

Source: McKinsey (2014).

different steps. The following describes the sustainability investment steps that can be applied to a thematic portfolio construction process:

Basic exclusions

- The investment firm or asset owner might apply a formal firm-wide exclusion list (e.g., manufacturers of controversial weapons).

Sustainable theme universe definition

- A minimum threshold of exposure to the theme is determined to include a company in the theme's investment universe. If the theme is a sustainable topic, this step ensures that all stocks in the portfolio are "doing the right thing."

- Theme-related activities deemed unsustainable can be excluded from investment universes (e.g., coal excluded from clean energy, weapons excluded from security).

ESG integration

- Environmental, social, and governance-related information can be formally integrated into the fundamental analyses of stocks, thereby impacting their weights in thematic portfolios. This ensures that companies "doing things right" are favoured.

Table 8. Selection of Sustainable Thematic Strategies Developed over the Last Two Decades

Sustainable Themes	Sustainability Challenge Addressed by Investing in Companies Developing Solutions in the Following Areas:
Water	Global water scarcity and quality crisis
Security	Improved personal safety and security in daily lives
Nutrition	Reducing the global food production imbalance
Healthy Living	Improved health
Forestry	Sustainable forestry management
Education	Access to information and educational technologies
Climate Change	Mitigate and adapt to climate change
Clean Energy	Accelerating the energy transition to a low-carbon economy
Biotech	Treatment and cure of rare diseases
Real Estate	Building energy-efficient housing

Active ownership

- A proxy voting policy might be in place to ensure that votes are exercised for all shares in thematic portfolios.

- An engagement policy might be implemented with the aim of improving investees' long-term performances and sustainability profiles.

Reporting on sustainability KPIs

- Some KPIs linked to the themes, as well as integrated ESG criteria, can be quantified and reported at the portfolio level (e.g., water savings, CO_2 avoided, employment created).

When contemplating the extensiveness of the approach described above, it becomes evident that thematic investing can be a strong sustainable investment strategy.

A wide spectrum of thematic strategies has emerged, addressing challenges that are highly relevant for investors intending to be active participants in the development of a sustainable society (**Table 8**).

Conclusion

Over the last 20 years, considerable experience has been gained in the area of sustainable thematic investing. Long-term superior risk-adjusted returns can be achieved while providing interesting diversification characteristics for institutional investors. The number of sustainable themes has multiplied, and some managers have now moved beyond simply investing in theme-exposed companies to fully integrating and reporting on ESG factors, proving that thematic investing can be an effective sustainable investment approach.

Endnotes

[1]In its most general definition, thematic investing is not confined to a specific asset class. Clean tech private equity, microfinance, or green bonds can be interpreted as forms of thematic investing as they focus on very specific segments of the economy. Today, however, the vast majority of thematic investment solutions are found in the form of public equity portfolios, which provide the daily liquidity that most investors look for. In this chapter, the discussion is limited to listed equities.

[2]Pictet limits its discussion to active management, as it is particularly well adapted to the dynamic nature of thematic universes.

[3]In standard global equity investing, managers typically use a global index as a benchmark. They then make active decisions to overweight or underweight individual stocks versus the chosen benchmark. Benchmarks are not used in thematic investing.

13. Impact Investing

Dr. Falko Paetzold
Managing Director, Center for Sustainable Finance and Private Wealth, University of Zurich

History and Definition

The concept of impact investing developed out of "*blended value*" in the 90s in the US, wherein thought leaders together with different organisations sought options to merge financial returns and philanthropic efforts. The term "impact investing" was coined during such a conversation convened by the Rockefeller Foundation in 2007.

The Rockefeller Foundation then initiated the Global Impact Investing Network (GIIN) in 2009, an association that by 2017 had established itself as a global network of over 200 organisations active in impact investing, including asset owners, asset managers, and service providers. One of its key outputs is an annual survey to collect information on volumes and trends within the impact investing space. As of 2017, the 208 respondents to the annual GIIN survey managed USD114 billion in impact investment assets.[1]

GIIN defines impact investing as investments made into companies, organisations, and funds with the intention to generate social and environmental impact alongside a financial return. Depending on investors' strategic goals, impact investments can be made in both industrialised and developing markets and deliver a range of financial returns, from market-rate to below-market rate (see **Figure 14**).

Further, a set of core characteristics helps to distinguish impact investments from other types of sustainable investing:

Intentionality refers to investees that, through the core activities of their business, specifically *intend to achieve a positive social or environmental impact*. Examples include health care services for underserved populations, education technologies, or social housing.

Measurability refers to the commitment and ability to measure and report the social and environmental outcomes of investees' business activities. This is done through systematic setting of social and environmental goals as well as performance metrics, monitoring, and reporting processes. The GIIN provides a standardised set of impact performance metrics through the IRIS[2] metrics catalogue. IRIS metrics, as well as other impact measuring frameworks, are widely applied by impact investors and funds globally. Building

Figure 14. Differentiating Impact Investing Based on Regional Focus and Expected Financial Return

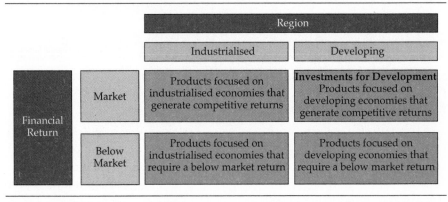

		Region	
		Industrialised	Developing
Financial Return	Market	Products focused on industrialised economies that generate competitive returns	**Investments for Development** Products focused on developing economies that generate competitive returns
	Below Market	Products focused on industrialised economies that require a below market return	Products focused on developing economies that require a below market return

Source: Swiss Sustainable Finance (2016).

upon the catalogue of IRIS performance metrics is the GIIRS rating system. GIIRS is a standardised, externally verified rating framework that is applied by many impact funds and investors.

Range of return expectations, regions, and asset classes. Impact investments cover a range of asset classes, from real estate (e.g., social housing), to fixed income (e.g., consolidated portfolios of micro-loans), to private equity/debt (e.g., clean tech in Germany). However, the majority of impact investment opportunities are based in developing markets in the form of primary-market investments and private equity/debt, venture capital, and real estate. This is due to the *intentionality* and *measurability* characteristics outlined above (and additionality, described next). These characteristics are less feasible in secondary markets and in listed equities in particular, where shares are sold from one investor to the other and the impact of deployed investor capital is more difficult to measure.

One aspect not mentioned by GIIN but to which advanced impact investors also pay close attention is the *additionality* of their investment capital: actively seeking to optimise the catalytic effect that the deployed capital has. These impact investors invest in funds, firms, or projects that would not have been realised *were it not for that particular capital being deployed*. Examples include anchor investments into first-time funds, or directly into the fund management companies themselves, or into such novel investment structures as social impact bonds (SIBs). Other examples include investments into particularly underserved (i.e., capital-starved) technologies, populations, or markets. An example would be a sanitation-infrastructure developer (technology) focused on rural bottom-of-the-pyramid farmers (population) in Rwanda

Figure 15. Impact Investing in the Spectrum of Sustainable Investment

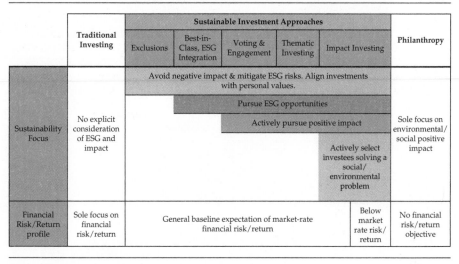

Source: Illustration by author.[3]

(market). Put differently, allocating capital into over-subscribed funds or projects that attract sufficient mainstream capital would be less interesting for these investors, who would rather aim to allocate their capital into funds or projects where their capital would be *additional*.

As such, investors can consider impact investing as the investment approach within the spectrum of sustainable investment approaches that is closest to philanthropy in terms of the focus on achieving a positive impact while still aiming for the full range of financial risk/returns, depending on investor preferences (see **Figure 15**).

Social and Environmental Impact Topics

Solutions to environmental or social challenges historically are obtained through public services or through philanthropy. Impact investors, however, aim for business models that deploy market-based solutions to social or environmental challenges.

As such, a key societal contribution of impact investing is to develop market-based solutions for many themes that historically were closed for the capital streams from investors that seek, at a minimum, the return of their capital.

Investors' interests in specific impact themes vary depending on investors' background, organisational set-up, and mandate. Banks deploy surveys and interviews to explore the interests of their clients.[4]

Figure 16. Investors' Planned Change of Capital Allocation for 2015 by Impact Themes

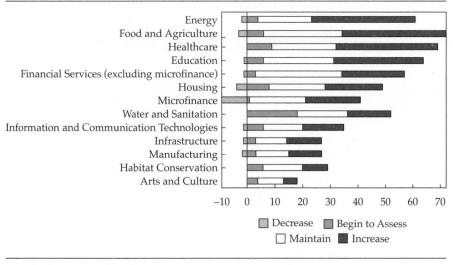

Note: Ranking by number of respondents who choose "increase".
Source: Saltuk, Y., & El Idrissi, A. (2015). *Eyes on the horizon.* J.P. Morgan & GIIN.

Investors' interests change over time. A survey by J.P. Morgan and GIIN in 2015 showed that the impact areas that received most interest for further allocations were food & agriculture, health care, education, and, since 2015, energy. Microfinance, a cornerstone of impact investing, is the only area where some investors planned to reduce allocations (see **Figure 16**).

A perspective on the focus of funds on specific impact topics can be gained through analysis of ImpactBase, the database managed by GIIN of more than 400 impact investing funds. Funds in ImpactBase indicate which of six impact themes they cover (one fund can cover multiple themes): Access to basic services, access to finance, employment generation, environmental markets and sustainable real assets (SRA), green technology, sustainable consumer products, and other themes. As per 2017, access to finance was the most prominent impact theme covered by impact investing funds. The theme includes mostly micro-finance and lending to small- and medium-size enterprises (SMEs). Access to basic services, the second most prominent impact theme, includes mostly solutions providing access to health care, education, clean energy, water, and sanitation.

In terms of allocation of capital across markets and themes, roughly half of AuM are deployed in developed markets (with social housing in the US playing a significant role), while half of AuM are deployed in developing markets (in particular in energy and microfinance) (GIIN, 2017).

Figure 17.   Performance Relative to Expectations

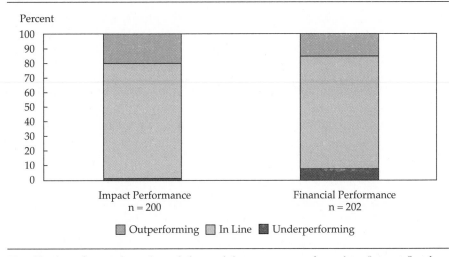

Note: Number of respondents shown below each bar, some respondents chose "not sure" and are not included.
Source: GIIN (2017).

Financial and Impact Performance

The majority of impact investing funds target the delivery of at least market-rate returns. This allows them to fully cater to the majority of investors, who equally expect market-rate returns.[5] Most impact investors are satisfied with the financial performance as well as the impact performance of their impact investments (**Figure 17**).

Data regarding the achieved financial performance of private debt/equity impact investing funds are still rare. Two studies, published by Wharton (2015) and GIIN/Cambridge Associates (2015), indicated that impact investing funds produce attractive financial returns and funds that outperform the benchmark exist. Both studies had small sample sizes (Wharton: 53 funds; GIIN/Cambridge: 36 funds) that differed in their characteristics from the market benchmark. However, their findings suggest that investors, depending on their preferences, do not need to compromise their financial return expectations. For example, micro-finance funds offer diversification of assets across millions of lenders in developing or frontier markets. This provided attractive and stable returns throughout the last financial crises and the current low-interest-rate environment (see also chapter 13.2 on microfinance).

Conclusion

With regard to financial risk, impact investing can provide diversification opportunities through engagements in populations and regions that offer largely uncorrelated returns relative to mainstream capital markets. Considering their core objective of actively seeking to contribute to positive social and environmental change while at a minimum aiming for return of their capital, impact investments represent a growing market for investors with a strong motivation to create continuous impact through their investments.

Further Reading

- Battilana, J., Kimsey, M., Paetzold, F., & Zogbi, P. (2017). *Vox Capital: Pioneering impact investing in Brazil.* Harvard Business School Case 417–051.

- Gray, J., Ashburn, N., Douglas, H., & Jeffers, J. (2015). *Great expectations: Mission preservation and financial performance in impact investing.* Wharton Social Impact Initiative of the University of Pennsylvania.

- Matthews, J., Sternlicht, D., Bouri, A., Mudaliar, A., & Schiff, H. (2015). *Introducing the impact investing benchmark.* GIIN & Cambridge Associates.

- Mudaliar, A., Schiff, H., Bass, R., & Dithrich, H. (2017). *Annual impact investor survey.* Global Impact Investing Network (GIIN).

- World Economic Forum. (WEF). *Impact investing: Primer for family offices.* Available at: weforum.org/reports/impact-investing-primer-family-offices.

Endnotes

[1]Mudaliar, A., Schiff, H., Bass, R., & Dithrich, H. (2017). *Annual impact investor survey.* Global Impact Investing Network (GIIN).

[2]https://iris.thegiin.org/.

[3]Partly adapted from Barby, C., & Goodall, E. (2014). Building impact-drive investment portfolios. In *From ideas to practice, Pilots to Strategy II.* World Economic Forum.

[4]UBS, for example, in 2011 reported that many of its clients were interested in supporting SMEs (especially clients with an entrepreneurial background) and that Asian clients tend to focus on their home; the bank subsequently launched products that were focused on this combination. The UBS & Harvard Kennedy School study *From prosperity to purpose: Perspectives on philanthropy and social investment among wealthy individuals in Latin America* (published in 2015) identified the same home bias for UHNWIs in Latin America and subsequently launched related products.

[5]See Mudaliar et al. (2017).

13.1. Investments for Development

Christian Etzensperger
Head of Corporate Strategy & Chief of Staff, responsAbility Investments AG

Scope

Investments for development are return-oriented investments in private companies whose inclusive business models benefit broad sections of the population in emerging and developing countries. They focus on sectors whose services are essential for any society's prosperity: finance, energy and climate adaption, agriculture, education, health care, water and sanitation, or housing (see **Figure 18**).

Hundreds of millions of emerging end-consumers constitute a source of relentless demand growth.[1] Private companies capture that demand by offering goods and services that end-clients judge superior to the available alternatives. One example is how domestic solar systems are profitably replacing kerosene and other unhealthy fossil energy sources. Highly scalable business models offer enormous growth potential given population size. However, most companies are unlisted and can be accessed only by direct investment.[2]

Figure 18.   Investments for Development by Sector (USD millions)

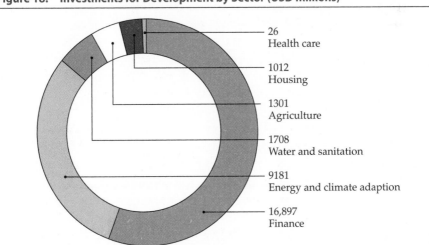

26
Health care

1012
Housing

1301
Agriculture

1708
Water and sanitation

9181
Energy and climate adaption

16,897
Finance

Sources: GIIN ImpactBase, Preqin, Symbiotics MIV Survey.

By attracting private capital, companies can offer new products and services to underserved end-clients, which strengthens sectors critical for a country's development. This enhanced offering results in general development and prosperity as well as in the companies' commercial success, which, in turn, benefits investors through an adequate financial return.[3]

Market

A survey of databases[4] reveals a market size of USD30 billion of assets under management by development investment intermediaries. The segment has grown over 20% per annum during the past decade. Switzerland is a leading global hub of investments for development, with USD9 billion of assets under management.[5] Going forward, such investments are likely to benefit strongly from both the Paris Agreement[6] and the Sustainable Development Goals,[7] given the bold commitments by governments and large private sector actors.

Underlying Instruments

Investments for development typically come in simple and transparent structures and offer market-rate returns. Products are either purely fixed-income, equity, or any blend of the two. The underlying investment instruments are principally private debt and private equity.

Debt investments consist of senior or subordinated debt. There is an emerging, but still very limited, market for secondary transactions. In most cases, the investor is offered limited liquidity with monthly or quarterly redemptions. Currency exposure can be hedged even for exotic currencies.

Private equity investments are usually structured as limited partnerships or holding companies. Optimal holding periods tend to be longer on average than in developed markets as book value development by business model execution is the dominant value driver. Industry experience shows longer holding periods can be in the interest of both general partners/sponsors,[8] on the one hand, and limited partners/investors, on the other.[9]

Average transaction sizes of both debt and equity instruments have increased strongly with sector development in emerging economies. In the financial sector, for instance, private equity transactions of USD2–5 million in microfinance institutions were common. Over the years, the respective institutions have grown, and today transaction sizes are around USD20 million. The strong growth in transaction sizes requires successful sequencing and up-scaling of closed-end funds (funds with defined time scales) or adjustable open-end structures (funds without a defined time scale).

Investment Themes

Thematically, the products can focus on a single sector, several defined sectors, or can be sector-agnostic. Investment teams typically focus on one sector as the analysis of sector-specific business models and the assessment of their implementation by skilful entrepreneurs on location is crucial. Investors can support a business model breakthrough by financing multiple companies in a market. This was seen in the microfinance industry, where investors contributed to creating large-scale development benefits through industry building.[10] Similar patterns of industries fostered by investments for development are also emerging in other sectors.

The principal sectors attracting investments for development are:

- **Finance:** Financial services for micro-, small-, and medium-sized enterprises (SMEs) as well as low-income households, including microfinance, SME banking, and micro-insurance

- **Energy and climate adaptation:** Production of clean energy, access to clean energy, reduction of carbon emissions, and climate change adaptation

- **Water and sanitation:** Access to safe drinking water and sanitation, water conservation

- **Agriculture:** sustainable agricultural production, domestic processing, food security

- **Housing:** Access to quality and affordable housing

- **Health care:** Health services and access to medicine

- **Education:** Enhanced academic opportunities and quality of education

The first sector to attract large volumes of development investments was finance. Financial institutions play a key role in economic development and should develop first, facilitating the growth of real-economy sectors. While some institutional investors were early adopters of microfinance, many more followed at the beginning of this decade once a multi-year performance track record was established. Today, microfinance is a mainstay of institutional investments for development. Other sectorial investment themes, such as energy or agriculture, have developed more recently and are now attracting increasing volumes of institutional assets.[11] In all sectors, private investors today benefit from decades of groundbreaking work by public development finance (by large development finance institutions (DFI), such as IFC, EBRD, or KfW). The geographical target markets of development investments are diversified over more than 100 countries in Latin America, Africa, and Asia.

Providers

As the underlying investment instruments are sourced locally and directly, market proximity is key. The quality of transaction sourcing is crucial, and due diligence is difficult to perform from a desk so should happen on site. Therefore, the larger investment managers operate global sourcing platforms empowering local specialists to process transactions in accordance with active portfolio management requirements. Specialised providers in Switzerland can be found on the Swiss Sustainable Finance website.[12] Their offering is increasingly differentiated across themes, instruments, return characteristics, and size (see **Table 9**).

Relevance for Institutional Investors

The emergence of investable and scalable companies in fast-growing market segments of developing countries and improved access to them constitute investment opportunities with market returns. Moreover, these returns are modestly to minimally correlated with most other assets investors usually hold in their portfolios. This is due to the fact that private debt or private equity investments in unlisted companies rooted in the real economy are hardly affected by the swings in global financial markets.

The expanded investment universe provided by investments for development offers additional and mostly uncorrelated risk premiums,[13] although in some cases at the cost of lower liquidity than other assets. These result in a higher investor portfolio diversification and hence a superior asset allocation in terms of both risk and return. The low correlation is partially explained by technical reasons, namely infrequent valuation or valuation at cost. Furthermore, investments for development effectively mitigate any "home bias," or the tendency of investors to concentrate investments in their country of residence. Therefore, investments for development should be represented in any investment portfolio.

Value from Values

A trend in society towards more sustainability in all aspects of life has only just started to permeate the financial markets. Asset owners can make a major contribution to boosting development and alleviating poverty by allocating capital to places where it is scarce and highly effective. Through their investments, they empower local entrepreneurship, which provides the solutions to many of the problems common to poor households.

Asset owners, such as endowments and foundations, increasingly seek to invest in accordance with their values, motivated by their boards or members. The same holds true for pension funds accountable to their stakeholders'

Table 9. Examples of "Swiss Made" Investments for Development Products

Fund Theme	Description	Instrument	Investors	Average Target Rate of Return (gross)	Size
Energy and climate adaption	Mitigates climate change through a reduction of greenhouse gas emissions by financing energy efficiency and renewable energy projects	Private debt/ mezzanine capital	Institutional investors and DFI	10–15%	USD100–500 million
Financial institutions	Takes long-term private equity positions in financial intermediaries with a solid track record of providing financial services to low-income groups, micro enterprises, or SMEs	Private equity	Institutional investors	15–25%	USD100–500 million
Financial institutions	Provides private debt financing to financial intermediaries with a solid track record of providing financial services to low-income groups, micro enterprises, or SMEs	Private debt	Institutional and private investors	3–6%	USD250 million– 1 billion
Education	Funds customised financial services for the education sector in a demand-oriented and financially sustainable manner	Private debt	Institutional investors and DFI	2–5%	USD100–200 million (target)
Climate insurance	Contributes to the adaptation to climate change by improving access to and the use of insurance in developing countries	Private debt or equity	Institutional investors and DFI	2–5%	USD100–200 million (target)
Multisector equity	Is set up as a limited partnership and invests in commercially viable companies that deliver essential goods and services that directly benefit low-income communities by providing access to affordable housing, health care, education, energy, livelihood opportunities, water, and sanitation	Private equity	Institutional and private investors	15–25%	USD100–200 million (target)
Multisector fund-of-funds	Serves as a multi-strategy product investing in a number of different themes, markets, regions, and asset classes— with a 60% fixed income, 30% high yield, and 10% equity breakdown target	Private debt, private equity	Institutional and private investors	10–15%	USD100–200 million (target)

Source: Analysis of provider websites; responsAbility Investments AG (2015).

growing interest in how assets are allocated.[14] Given their size and level of influence, institutional investors play a central role in how capital is deployed. Long-term investors will not only see companies grow but also will see the building of entire industries catering to large populations of emerging consumers. This was clearly observed over the last decade of financial sector development.[15]

Investor Horizon and Impact

Private equity offers the possibility to exercise direct influence on the development and growth of a company. As development does not happen in the short term but requires time, private equity is an ideal investment as a development instrument. The impact of fixed-income investors tends to be less profound but broader as large volumes can be deployed over many investees. Private debt excels with performance stability thanks to diversification over several dozen countries, and it allows tactical adjustments.

Asset Classification

In recent years, private debt (e.g., in the topic of microfinance debt funds) was often classified as "fixed-income emerging markets" due to the stable return characteristics and thus allocated to the fixed-income asset class by pension funds. In most cases, however, investments for development fall into the "alternative investments" asset class, a trend that has increased since the revised BVV 2 regulation came into force in 2015. Since 2009, Swiss pension funds are subject to a 15% limit for alternative assets,[16] which is why investments for development often stand in harsh competition with other alternative asset classes, some of them with higher target returns. However, an extension of this limit (e.g., to include investments for development) is explicitly foreseen by the law.

Conclusions

Investments for development have become highly relevant for institutional investors due to their track record demonstrating attractive return characteristics over more than 10 years. Swiss asset owners and investment practitioners understood and seized the opportunity early on and have contributed to re-route capital to where it is most effective. Real and perceived regulatory hurdles must not discourage the turning of pressing societal concerns, such as climate change, into investment opportunities.

Further Reading

- Balandina Jaquier, J. (2016). *Catalyzing wealth for change: Guide to impact investing*. Available at: https://www.guidetoimpactinvesting.net/.

- Global Impact Investing Network (GIIN). (2016). *Homepage.* https://the-giin.org/.

- Swiss Sustainable Finance & University of Zurich. (2016). *Swiss investments for a better world: The first market survey on investments for development.* Available at: http://www.sustainablefinance.ch/upload/cms/user/SSF_A4_Layout_RZ-1.pdf.

Endnotes

[1]Ravallion, M. (2015). *The economics of poverty: History, measurement and policy.* Oxford: Oxford University Press.

[2]Wendt, K. (Ed.). (2015). *Responsible investment banking—Risk management frameworks, sustainable financial innovation and softlaw standards.* Berlin: Springer.

[3]Ibid.

[4]GIIN ImpactBase, Preqin, Symbiotics MIV Survey, company websites.

[5]Swiss Sustainable Finance & University of Zurich. (2016). *Swiss investments for a better world.* Available at: http://www.sustainablefinance.ch/upload/cms/user/SSF_A4_Layout_RZ-1.pdf.

[6]The agreement was negotiated during the 21st Conference of the Parties of the UN Framework Convention on Climate Change in Paris and adopted by consensus on 12 December 2015.

[7]The Sustainable Development Goals are an intergovernmental agreement adopted by the UN General Assembly on 25 September 2015.

[8]The sponsor is the party that has the General Partner/Limited Partner structure set-up and thus becomes the sponsor of the General Partner. The General Partner is a specially established entity that implements the investment programme and is made up of separate Limited Partners, which only engage financially.

[9]Olds, P. (2015). *Emerging markets fund terms—How and why do they differ from developed markets funds?* Cleary Gottlieb Steen & Hamilton LLP. Available at: https://www.empea.org/research/emerging-markets-fund-terms-how-and-why-do-they-differ-from-developed-markets-funds/.

[10]Roodman, D. (2012). *Due diligence: An impertinent inquiry into microfinance.* London: CGD Books.

[11]Emerson, J. (Ed.). (2016). *Social finance.* Oxford: Oxford University Press.

[12]Swiss Sustainable Finance. (2016). *Homepage.* Available at: http://www.sustainablefinance.ch/.

[13]Zaugg, B. (2011). *Chancen und Risiken von Mikrofinanzanlagen aus anlagestrategischer Sicht.* Zürich: Ecofin.

[14]Clark, C., Emerson, J., & Thornley, B. (2014). *The Impact investor: Lessons in leadership and strategy for collaborative capitalism.* Hoboken, NJ: John Wiley & Sons.

[15]Roodman, D. (2012). *Due diligence: An impertinent inquiry into microfinance.* London: CGD Books.

[16]Verordnung über die berufliche Alters-, Hinterlassenen- und Invalidenvorsorge (BVV2) (Ordinance on Occupational Old Age, Survivors' and Invalidity Pension Provision, OPO2), Article 50, Paragraph 4.

13.2. Microfinance

Marina Parashkevova
Research Team Leader, Symbiotics SA

Fabio Sofia
Head of Portfolio Advisory, Symbiotics SA

Two billion people in the world lack access to formal financial services. This represents a major impediment in the struggle to lift people out of poverty, as recent empirical evidence suggests that access to basic financial services is positively correlated with growth and employment.[1] Accordingly, financial sector reforms that promote financial inclusion are increasingly at the core of policymakers' agendas worldwide. The United Nations has also included this as an integral part of the United Nations Sustainable Development Goals.[2]

Microfinance is the provision of financial services to micro and small enterprises and low-income households in emerging economies by specialised financial institutions. Worldwide, there are estimates of more than 10,000 financial institutions serving more than 250 million clients living mostly in developing economies. About 500 of these institutions are large, mature, and profitable and are frequently regulated by local authorities. They often attract international funding through Microfinance Investment Vehicles (MIVs).

According to the Symbiotics MIV Survey,[3] there are 110 specialised MIVs worldwide that have grown at a steady rate of 5% per year for the last four years and managed assets of USD10.4 billion as of December 2014. With USD3.9 billion (i.e., 38% of the global market) in assets (managed or advised), Switzerland is the world leader in microfinance investments, attracting not only institutional investors (57%) but also retail investors (23.5%), public sources (14.7%), and high-net-worth individuals (3.7%). The majority of products offered are fixed income with an average investment size of USD2.2 million.

During the last decade, the Symbiotics Microfinance Index—the first industry benchmark aggregating and tracking the main global fixed-income funds that target microfinance institutions in developing countries—has demonstrated the strong resilience of this set of funds to global economic downturns, offering positive and stable returns of 2% to 6% in USD over the past 13 years (see **Figure 18a**).[4]

Figure 18a. Symbiotics Microfinance Index in US Dollars (SMX USD)

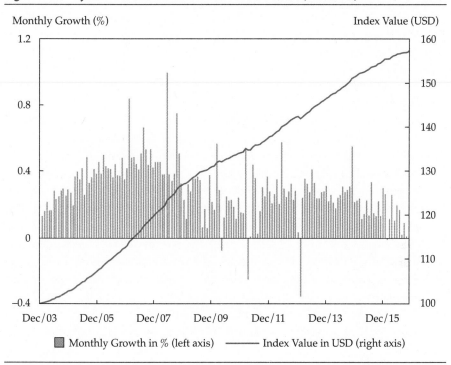

Monthly Growth (%)   Index Value (USD)

☐ Monthly Growth in % (left axis)   ——— Index Value in USD (right axis)

Endnotes

[1]Cull, R., Ehrbeck, T., & Holle, N. (2014). Financial inclusion and development: Recent impact evidence. *Focus Note, 92.*

[2]World Bank. (2015). *Massive drop in number of unbanked, says new report.* Available at: http://www.worldbank.org/en/news/press-release/2015/04/15/massive-drop-in-number-of-unbanked-says-new-report.

[3]Microfinance Investment Vehicles are independent investment entities that specialise in microfinance, with more than 50% of their non-cash assets invested in microfinance.

[4]The SMX-MIV Debt Index is a Symbiotics proprietary index. For more information, please visit www.syminvest.com.

14. Green Bonds

Catherine Reichlin
Head of Financial Research, Mirabaud & Cie.

Green bonds first appeared in 2007,[1] but it took almost seven years longer for the market linked to sustainable, climate-related projects to really develop. The first to be interested in green bonds were environmentally conscious investors and development banks, such as the World Bank and the EIB. In 2013, public authorities and companies brought momentum to the market, diversifying a business so far dominated by euro-denominated issues. Things really picked up speed in 2014, with the arrival of new issuers and more substantially sized borrowings. A major turning point was the issuance, by GDF Suez (now Engie), of a EUR2.5 billion bond to finance such projects as the construction of wind farms. The bond was oversubscribed almost three times, and 36% of the issue was bought by non-ESG investors, which was critical to "democratise" the field. It wasn't only energy companies that contributed to this ramp up. Unilever blazed a trail by issuing the first ever green bond to finance the reduction of its carbon footprint. After manufacturing came the finance industry—banks in particular—with governments finally getting involved fairly late in the game, with Poland and later France issuing bonds in 2016 and 2017, respectively.

What Makes a Bond "Green"?

One of the main, albeit not the sole, criteria is that the bond is issued exclusively to finance environmental projects. In 2014, given the growing interest for this market, banks and issuers adopted the Green Bond Principles and entrusted coordination of them to the International Capital Market Association (ICMA) in its capacity as governance body for capital markets. These non-binding principles have four core components:

- Use of Proceeds
- Process for Project Evaluation and Selection[2]
- Management of Proceeds
- Reporting

The Green Bond Principles have been updated each year since their inception, and the next update will need to take account of recent market experiences. Toyota, for example, issued a green bond for projects that had yet to be launched, and while waiting for the funds to be invested, the constructor placed the proceeds in money market funds that were not subject to ESG criteria. This incident highlighted the importance of being able to trace funds and their usage leading up to investment. The Green Bonds market is not easy to fool and is self-regulatory to a certain extent. The lack of official regulatory constraints does not mean that the market accepts everything claiming to be a green bond. In 2015, a Chinese corporation generating most of its revenues through renewable energies issued a self-designated green bond without links to any specific projects, traceability mechanisms, or relevant data transparency. ESG investors refused to recognise the bond as green. More recently, the oil company Repsol provided another telling example that fed into the green debate by seeking to raise funds to improve the energy efficiency of its refineries. The market was unwilling to qualify such a bond as green, and therefore it is not included in the green indices. Although the Green Bond Principles are updated each year, this example highlights the importance of better defining the criteria that enable projects to qualify as green.

Specialised rating agencies have emerged to assist issuers looking to release green bonds. Traditional rating agencies are now also surfing on the green bond wave and proposing their own specific green rating methods. Finally, there is the crucial issue of reporting, with a number of issuers now dedicating a chapter of their annual report to project tracking and the use of funds.

How Does a Green Bond Differ from a Traditional Bond?

The main difference between traditional and green bonds is how the funds are put to use. In the case of green bonds, funds must be used exclusively to finance environmental projects, with investors accordingly aware of which projects their funds have been allocated to.

Theoretically speaking there can be no yield spread between traditional and green bonds. In both cases, credit exposure arises from the same balance sheet and financial ratios and similar returns should thus be garnered by each. Green bonds are, therefore, a genuine investment vehicle as opposed to a form of philanthropy.

The green bond market is experiencing a tremendous upswing, setting new records each year. Several structural changes have taken place, in particular the increasing presence of the US dollar and such emerging markets as China and India in the wake of COP 21 as well as the onset of specialised indices and funds. In 2016, green bonds to the tune of USD81 billion, or almost USD10 million per hour, were issued. The market is looking just as dynamic for 2017, with close to USD56 billion issued in the first half of 2017[3] alone and almost half of second-quarter bonds being issued by new market arrivals.

Can the Market Continue to Grow?

Although the market is constantly expanding, certain questions remain unanswered. Should there be a legal framework surrounding selection criteria? How is environmental impact measured? Do standards need to be drawn up? Should governments incentivise companies to reduce their CO_2 emissions? The cost factor should also be examined, with green bonds costing companies more than traditional loans due to specific rating, traceability, and reporting requirements.

In 2015, historic decisions were made in favour of this promising market. In June, the G7 voted to cut greenhouse gas emissions by 40% to 70% by 2050. Green bonds therefore appeared to be an ideal financing tool, and certain players were of the opinion that they would even represent between 10% and 15% of total bond issues by 2020. The wheels are in motion, with green bonds already accounting for 3% by Q2 2017. In December 2015, the Paris climate agreement, which marked the close of the COP 21, contributed to reaching the forecasts by attracting new players, such as China and India, to the table. The trend will not be jeopardised by Donald Trump's planned withdrawal from the agreement; indeed it has even highlighted the strength and commitment of the citizens with the launch of the emblematic "We are still in"[4] movement.

Further Reading

- Climate Bonds Initiative. (2016). *Bonds and climate change. The state of the market in 2016*. Available at: http://www.climatebonds.net/resources/publications/bonds-climate-change-2016.

- The World Bank. (2016). *Green bonds*. World Bank Green Bonds. Available at: http://treasury.worldbank.org/cmd/htm/What-are-Green-Bonds-Home.html.

- WWF. (2016). *Green bonds must keep the green promise! A call for collective action towards effective and credible standards for the green bond market*. Available at: http://d2ouvy59p0dg6k.cloudfront.net/downloads/20160609_green_bonds_hd_report.pdf.

Endnotes

[1]Climate Bonds Initiative. (2016). *History*. Available at: https://www.climatebonds.net/market/history.

[2]Non-exhaustive list of categories considered: renewable energy, energy efficiency (including buildings), sustainable waste management, sustainable use of land (including forestry and agriculture), biodiversity conservation, clean transport, sustainable water management, adaptation to climate change.

[3]Climate Bonds Initiative. (2017). *Climate Bond 2017, Highlights*. Available at: https://www.climatebonds.net/resources/reports/green-bonds-mid-year-summary-2017.

[4]http://wearestillin.com/.

15. Sustainable Infrastructure Investments

Katharina Schneider-Roos
CEO, Global Infrastructure Basel (GIB) Foundation

Basil Oberholzer
Project Manager, Financial Services, GIB Foundation

Investments in infrastructure—such as transport networks, waste recycling plants, drinking water and wastewater treatment facilities, and electricity generation plants—provide the backbone for economic and social development. According to the OECD, demand for infrastructure investments will amount to more than USD70 trillion, equivalent to 3.5% of predicted global GDP, by 2030. In financing this enormous demand for infrastructure, private capital plays an increasingly important role, both in Switzerland and abroad.

Certain characteristics of infrastructure projects make them attractive investment opportunities for a growing number of private investors. The main reasons are the following:

- Attractive returns (see **Figure 19**) combined with high and stable cash flows. The EBITDA[1] of global infrastructure investments exceeds 7.5% p.a. (AMP Capital, 2014).

- Performance is resilient to economic cycles and in some cases linked to inflation (Af2i and J.P. Morgan Asset Management, 2011).

- Low correlation with other asset classes, such as equities, bonds, and commodities (Credit Suisse, 2010).

- Competitive advantages due to high market entry barriers.

Determining factors of the appeal of this asset class lie in a) the choice of a project, b) the quality of a project, and c) the associated risk. If consideration is also given to ESG criteria as complementary factors in the planning, construction, and operation of infrastructure projects, the basis for making a decision on these three aspects can be improved and the attraction increased even further.

In order to apply ESG criteria, such as resource and energy efficiency, to an infrastructure project, key ESG areas for the project need to be identified along with their requirements, feasibility, and potential (ESG Handbook, 2015). The ESG criteria vary depending on the location and type of project and should be integrated into project development as early as possible so as to

Figure 19. Performance of Different Asset Classes (in local currency in %)

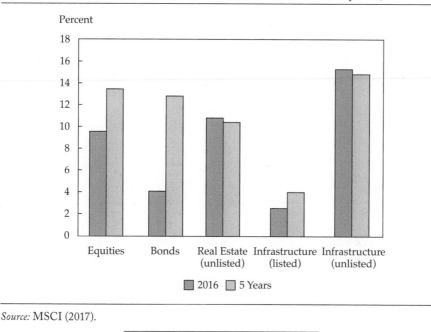

Source: MSCI (2017).

maximise their effect. Other examples of ESG criteria include: sustainable building materials, waste reduction, emissions reduction, job creation, flood resilience, biodiversity, and corporate governance.

In order to identify ESG criteria, investors can refer to such general methods as the International Finance Corporation (IFC) Performance Standards or the UN-supported Principles for Responsible Investment (PRI), such infrastructure-specific instruments as GRESB (the Global ESG Benchmark for Real Assets) or SuRe® (the Standard for Sustainable and Resilient Infrastructure), and can also use internal ESG checklists.

Scientific studies analysing the correlation between ESG and infrastructure performance are not yet available due to the limited amount of existing relevant data. However, numerous case studies highlight the superior performance and underline the importance of ESG factors for infrastructure investments:

- **Risk mitigation:** Consideration of ESG criteria helps anticipate and reduce risks before they cause losses or costs. In addition, a lower risk of future losses also implies a lower credit default risk. This reduces the amount of interest costs on infrastructure investments.

- **Cost reduction:** The efficient and effective use of energy, building materials, and resources reduces the level of consumption and results in lower building and annual operating costs.

- **Greater business stability:** Incorporating the needs of stakeholders and using cutting-edge technologies make infrastructure investments more future-proof and generally enable smoother operation over the entire life cycle.

Table 10. Advantages and Disadvantages of Various Forms of Infrastructure Investments

Investment	Advantages	Disadvantages
Listed funds	• Liquidity • Relatively low transaction costs • Market prices (mark-to-market) • Simple access • Greater security due to tighter regulation • Low investment volume allowed	• Greater volatility and higher correlation with other asset classes, as listed funds invest not only directly in infrastructure projects but also in actual construction companies • Focus on share price can encourage short-term perspective
Unlisted funds	• General Partnership (GP) structures the investment and manages the risk • GP can have direct influence on business operations and the management • No real-time "mark-to-market" volatility	• Mostly high management fees and running costs • Limited liquidity and transparency • Periodic valuation (mark-to-model) • Capital employed is locked in for several years (5–10 years)
Funds-of-funds	• Maximum diversification by incorporating several GPs • Focus on risk management and financial soundness • Chance for co-investments and secondary purchases • Smallest investment volume possible	• Management fees and running costs • Limited liquidity • Capital employed is locked in for several years (5–10 years)
Direct investments	• Direct (whole or partial) ownership of the project • Significant influence possible on project development	• Large investment volume • Intensive management and know-how required • Owner carries risk

- **Improved sustainability:** The integration of resilience criteria[2] and the optimal allocation of resources also make an infrastructure project more sustainable and, for example, improve its resilience to the growing number of natural catastrophes caused by climate change (Intergovernmental Panel on Climate Change, IPCC).

There are four main options for investors interested in infrastructure, whether conventional or sustainable: listed funds, unlisted funds, funds-of-funds, and direct investments (see **Table 10**).

Successfully integrating ESG criteria into the infrastructure investment allows certain risks to be minimised, on the one hand, and the attraction of these investments to be improved, on the other hand. Furthermore, sustainable and resilient infrastructure projects make a significant contribution to the attainment of the United Nations Sustainable Development Goals (SDGs) due to their positive social and environmental impacts.

Further Reading

- AMP Capital & Consilia Capital. (2014). *Infrastructure investment: Combining listed with unlisted.* Available from: https://www.ampcapital.com/site-assets/articles/insights-papers/2014/2014-10/infrastructure-investment-combining-listed-with-un.

- Credit Suisse. (2010). *Können Infrastrukturanlagen die Portfolioeffizienz erhöhen? (Can infrastructure investments improve portfolio efficiency?)* (German only). Available from: https://www.credit-suisse.com/pwp/am/downloads/marketing/white_paper_infrastructure_ch_ger.pdf.

- Deutsche Asset & Wealth Management. (2014). *Why invest in infrastructure.* Available from: http://infrastructure.deutscheam.com/content/_media/Research_Deutsche_AWM_Why_Invest_in_Infrastructure_May_2015.pdf.

- ICLEI—Local Governments for Sustainability. (2016). *Our library.* Available from: http://www.ltiia.org/library/.

- Long-Term Infrastructure Investors Association. (2015). *Environmental, Social and Governance Handbook for Long Term Investors in Infrastructure.* Available from: http://www.gib-foundation.org/content/uploads/2016/03/LTIIA-ESG-Handbook-Excerpts.pdf.

- MSCI. (2017). *MSCI Global Quarterly Infrastructure Asset Index: Consultative release.* Available from: https://support.msci.com/documents/1296102/0e192d3c-bbfb-4e3a-958f-8ba934d2d848.

- UBS Global Asset Management. (2012). *An introduction to infrastructures as an asset class*. New York: UBS.

- Weber B., & Wilhelm-Alfen, H. (2010). *Infrastructure as an asset class: Investment strategies, project finance and PPP*. Chichester: Wiley.

Endnotes

[1]EBITDA: Earnings before interest, taxes, depreciation, and amortisation.
[2]Resilience here refers to the ability of infrastructure to withstand and regenerate in the event of a sudden catastrophe or crisis (Center for Security Studies CSS, ETH Zurich).

16. Sustainable Private Equity Investments

Adam Heltzer
Responsible Investment, Partners Group

Development of Sustainable Investment in Private Equity

Most investors wanting to take account of environmental, social, and governance (ESG) factors focused initially on listed equities investments. However, when it comes to managing ESG factors effectively, private equity investors have inherent corporate governance advantages compared to their public market peers. These provide opportunities to implement superior sustainable investment strategies and to enhance investment returns (see **Figure 20**).[1]

Private equity investors are increasingly recognising the expectation and opportunity for them to invest sustainably and are leveraging these inherent advantages. Currently, nearly 300 signatories to the UN-supported Principles for Responsible Investment (PRI) invest in private equity.

Implementation

In private equity, there are three different types of investments:

Figure 20. **Comparison of Corporate Governance of Private Equity and Public Market Investors**

	Private investors	Public investors
Information	**Detailed:** full access to information on firms during due diligence and ownership	**Limited:** Limited due diligence possible, only public information available to investors
Influence	**Large, concentrated shareholdings:** more control and better alignment of incentives	**Limited:** all UK FTSE 350 board director candidates proposed from 2006 to 2010 were approved by shareholders*
Time horizon	**Long-term ownership:** enables long-term approach to value creation. **Value creation focus**	**Short:** average duration of US & UK public investors' holdings has fallen to 7 months.** **Quarterly reporting focus.**

Sources: *Cevian's submission to Kay Review (2011); **"Patience and Finance," speech by Andrew Haldane, Partners Group (2010).

1. **Direct:** an investment made directly by a private equity investor in a privately held company.

2. **Primary:** an investment made by an investor into a private equity fund (sometimes known as a "fund of funds").

3. **Secondary:** an investment made by one investor selling to another investor his holding in an asset or portfolio of assets part of the way through the term of the private equity fund.

The implementation of sustainable investment strategies varies between the different types of private equity investments, as illustrated in the "toolkit" below.

Direct investments. Direct investments offer investors greater control over their private equity portfolio companies.

- **Sourcing:** Environmental and social trends are powerful drivers of change and are thus linked to business opportunity. Private equity investors can, therefore, use such trends proactively to identify companies with promising growth prospects.

- **Due diligence:** During due diligence, direct private equity investors obtain full access to information on a company. They can use this to assess how the company is managing ESG factors and thereby identify:

    i. potential reputational or investment risks that could affect the attractiveness or valuation of the company, and

    ii. areas in which the company's management of ESG factors needs to be improved during the ownership period.

- **Acquisition:** Before investing, private equity investors can obtain warranties that a company is following relevant laws and standards. Governance arrangements, such as the composition of the board and management compensation, are also agreed at this stage.

- **Ownership:** Private equity investors are often represented on the boards of their portfolio companies. This enables them to actively initiate and complete projects, together with management teams, designed to improve how ESG factors are managed. Typically, the active investment manager will work closely with management teams to develop a company and increase its value throughout the life of the investment.

- **Exit:** Well-implemented projects that improve a company's management of ESG factors may facilitate a sales process and can even drive valuation.

Primary and secondary investments. The implementation of sustainable investment practices in primary and secondary investments requires investors to ensure investment managers are effectively integrating ESG factors.[2]

- **Primaries:** Prior to making a commitment, investors should perform thorough due diligence to ensure an investment manager has integrated ESG factors into the management of a private equity fund.[3] In addition, potential investors in a private equity fund often seek to negotiate ESG-related terms into the documentation that governs how the fund will be managed. In practice, this is generally achieved by including specific additional arrangements in the limited partnership agreement (the document that governs how the private equity fund will be managed). Finally, during the life of a private equity fund, investors can influence the investment manager via the fund's advisory board to ensure the portfolio companies manage ESG factors effectively.

- **Secondaries:** Private equity investors have good visibility on the assets in a portfolio when it comes to secondary investments and during due diligence and can, therefore, assess the underlying portfolios to identify companies that pose ethical or reputational risks. They can interact with the investment managers during ownership in the same way primary investors can, but they do not have the same ability to influence the initial terms that govern how a fund will operate.

Performance Impact and Societal Benefits

Leading investors, particularly in the US, have developed advanced metrics to measure the societal benefits of their private equity investments. Metrics can cover a range of environmental and social benefits. For example, the direct private equity investments led and jointly led by Partners Group had a net job creation rate of 3.6% during 2016, which was 2.6× greater than that achieved by the US economy in 2015.[4] Therefore, by providing an attractive risk–return profile and proven societal benefits, sustainable private equity investments could be preferred to other investments that do not integrate ESG factors as effectively.

Further Reading

- Principles for Responsible Investment. (2016). *Report on progress: Private equity.*

- Principles for Responsible Investment & Institutional Investors Group on Climate Change. (2016). *A guide on climate change for private equity investors.*

Endnotes

[1]Harris, R. S., Jenkinson, T., & Kaplan, S. N. (2014). Private equity performance: What do we know? *Journal of Finance, 69*(5), 1851–1882.

[2]In primary investments, the asset owners are known as Limited Partners (LPs) and the investment manager is known as the General Partner (GP).

[3]To enable more efficient and effective due diligence on primary investments, the United Nations-supported Principles for Responsible Investment published in December 2015 a "Limited Partner Due Diligence Questionnaire": https://www.unpri.org/news/pri-launches-private-equity-due-diligence-question.

[4]Furthermore, in the 12 months up to June 2016, Partners Group's direct infrastructure investments avoided 1,100,000 metric tons of carbon dioxide, enabled 2.7 million people to travel safely, and supplied 3.6 million people with water.

17. Sustainable Real Estate

Roger Baumann
COO & Head Sustainability, Credit Suisse Global Real Estate

The Market for Greener Buildings

At the global climate conference in Paris in December 2015, the international community agreed on a new climate protection accord to reduce harmful greenhouse gas emissions. Since buildings account for around 40% of global CO_2 emissions, sustainable real estate can make a significant contribution towards achieving global climate protection goals.[1]

"Green real estate" and "green buildings" have been gathering momentum as a theme in the real estate sector for some years and mirror the trend towards more sustainable properties. In Europe, there are now more green buildings being constructed than conventional buildings.[2] The same is true for the US commercial property market. Sustainable buildings account for between 40% and 48% of the total real estate market.[3] This is equivalent to an annual investment volume of around USD200 billion in 2016.[4] Up to USD300 billion is currently being invested in green buildings worldwide,[5] a trend that shows no sign of slowing down.

Sustainable properties can offer added value, as reflected in the higher rental and sales prices they achieve on national and international real estate markets (see **Figure 21**). Studies show that in some cases rental prices are more than 10% higher and sales prices up to 30% higher when compared with conventional properties.[6] Apart from financial factors, such as securing and enhancing the risk-adjusted return, the main advantages are environmental benefits, resulting from lower energy and resource consumption, as well as positive social aspects. Sustainable real estate therefore integrates environmental, social, and governance (ESG) factors into investment decisions. The general assumption is that sustainable properties are better equipped to meet the challenges of the future, help to reduce risks, and offer the prospect of superior returns. In addition, building regulations and disclosure obligations are getting stricter worldwide, turning green buildings into a necessity rather than a luxury.

Sustainability Certificates and Green Labels

Green buildings often carry sustainability certificates or labels that allow users to judge the quality of their sustainability performance. Certificates

Figure 21.   Market Studies Highlight Financial Success of Sustainable Real Estate

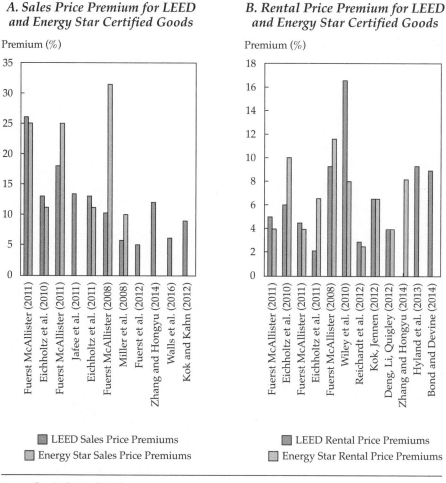

A. Sales Price Premium for LEED and Energy Star Certified Goods

B. Rental Price Premium for LEED and Energy Star Certified Goods

LEED Sales Price Premiums
Energy Star Sales Price Premiums

LEED Rental Price Premiums
Energy Star Rental Price Premiums

Source: Credit Suisse (2017).

are predominantly awarded to new buildings, often with a focus on energy and resource efficiency. Also, certification for existing properties is becoming increasingly common. Sustainability labels improve marketability, act as a control instrument, allow for better risk management, and offer competitive advantages. Finally, green labels signal real commitments in the area of corporate social responsibility and can contribute towards a positive image.

In Switzerland, the "Minergie" label is well established, with more than 44,000 certifications in total, and is used mainly for residential properties. Compared with other countries, the "Minergie" label is relatively widely distributed. Therefore, on a per-capita basis, Switzerland has a very high penetration rate of building certifications, compared to its international peers.[7]

Key Performance Indicators for Sustainable Real Estate

In addition to sustainability certificates, key performance indicators (KPIs) are used to measure the sustainability performance of green buildings.[8] The real estate sector therefore follows the international reporting standards of the Global Reporting Initiative (GRI), in conjunction with the Construction and Real Estate Sector Supplement (CRESS).[9] Key aspects measured include end energy consumption, primary energy use, CO_2 emissions, and water and waste consumption. From this basis, portfolio-specific and property-specific opportunities for optimisation can be derived.

Benchmarking Green Real Estate

Benchmarks have been established in order to assess the sustainability performance on a portfolio level in both national and international peer groups. Leading providers include the Global Real Estate Sustainability Benchmark (GRESB), which brings together over 700 participants for their assessment. In 2017, GRESB represented real estate worth more than USD3.7 trillion.[10] In Switzerland, all leading real estate companies and real estate asset managers already participate in the GRESB assessment. GRESB's goals are to make the real estate sector's sustainability performance more transparent and to improve it. End investors and real estate investors can thus monitor the sustainability performance of the asset managers and objectively assess their performance.

Sustainable or green real estate is increasingly becoming the default option. The transparency of the sustainability performance will continue to improve. To remain competitive, sustainability performance must be systematically reported and optimised.

Further Reading

- Faust, M., & Scholz, S. (Eds.). (2014). *Nachhaltige Geldanlagen: Produkte, Strategien und Beratungskonzepte*. Frankfurt: Frankfurt School Verlag.

- Schäfer, M. (9 June 2016). *Das bessere Betongold*. NZZ. Available here: https://www.nzz.ch/finanzen/immobilien/nachhaltige-immobilien-das-bessere-betongold-ld.87647.

- UNEP FI. (2016). *Sustainable real estate investment implementing the Paris Climate Agreement: An action framework*. Available here: http://www.unepfi.org/fileadmin/documents/SustainableRealEstateInvestment.pdf.

Endnotes

[1]International Energy Agency. (2016). *Homepage*. Available at: http://www.iea.org/.

[2]European Commission. (2013). *The European construction sector—A global partner*. Available here: http://www.efcanet.org/Portals/EFCA/EFCA%20files/PDF/The%20European%20construction%20sector_A%20global%20Partner_European%20Union_2014.pdf.

[3]Hamilton, B. A. (2015). *Green Building Economic Impact Study*. U.S. Green Building Council. Available at: http://go.usgbc.org/2015-Green-Building-Economic-Impact-Study.html.

[4]Wharton, The University of Pennsylvania. (2013). *The rapid rise of green building*. Available at: http://knowledge.wharton.upenn.edu/special-report/the-rapid-rise-of-green-building/.

[5]UNEP FI. (2016). Sustainable real estate investment implementing the Paris Climate Agreement: An action framework executive summary.

[6]Wiencke, A., & Enskog, D. (2015). *Green real estate—A significant value proposition*. Credit Suisse Research. Available at: https://www.credit-suisse.com/corporate/en/articles/news-and-expertise/green-real-estate-a-significant-value-proposition-201510.html.

[7]Minergie. (2017). *Homepage*. Available at: https://www.minergie.ch/.

[8]KPIs are best practice; see EPRA Best Practice Recommendations.

[9]Global Reporting Initiative. (2016). *Homepage*. Available at: https://www.globalreporting.org/Pages/default.aspx.

[10]Global Real Estate Sustainability Benchmark. (2017). *Homepage*. Available at: https://www.gresb.com/.

18. Integrating Sustainability into Commodity Investing

Alex Tobler, CFA
Head of Sustainable Investment, Berner Kantonalbank*

Dr. Marco Haase
Head of Research Sustainable Finance, Center for Corporate Responsibility and Sustainability (CCRS), University of Zurich

Peter Sigg
Senior Investment Strategist, LGT Capital Partners*

Introduction

Generally, commodity investments can be divided into direct and indirect investments. Direct investments include real productive assets, such as agricultural land or physical commodities (e.g., gold), whereas indirect investments include debt or equities from commodity-related companies and commodity derivatives (see **Figure 22**). A main discussion concerning commodity investments and ESG or sustainability issues revolves around the impact of physical and derivative investors on commodity prices. Numerous organisations and political parties claim that commodity investments influence commodity prices, especially food commodity prices, which may, in turn, adversely affect food security in developing countries. This chapter focuses on ESG issues related to physical and derivative commodity investing, while leaving aside investments in real productive assets as well as debt and equity investments in resource companies.[1]

Commodity Derivatives

Investing in commodity derivatives, which is done mainly via futures, is the most common way to gain commodity price exposure in an investor's portfolio without buying or selling the physical underlying.[3] Although investments are not directly made in physical markets, managers should still consider ESG issues. ESG concerns mainly relate to possible adverse effects

---

*Authors' Note: This chapter partially reflects the personal judgments of the authors and may not always be congruent with the opinions of Berner Kantonalbank or LGT Capital Partners.

Figure 22.   Commodity Investment Universe[2]

Investment Universe			
Direct		Indirect	
Real Productive Assets	Physical Commodities	Debt or Equity Investments	Commodity Derivatives
• Forest • Agricultural land	• Gold, silver • Aluminium, copper	• Mining companies • Oil producers	• Futures • OTC contracts • Index swaps

Source: Commodity Club Switzerland.

of financial investments on commodity futures and spot prices. As demonstrated by the world food price crisis in 2007 and 2008, strong agricultural price fluctuations may have adverse effects on food security with far-reaching implications for the political and economic stability of developing countries.[4] Therefore, a key target in the United Nations' 2030 Agenda for Sustainable Development is to limit food price volatility.[5] Strongly supported by accepted economic theory[6] and numerous empirical studies,[7] financial investors fulfil an important role in food security by their contribution to lower price volatility. They provide commercial hedgers[8] with the needed liquidity for insurance against price risk and improve the information efficiency of prices within the price discovery process. However; as suggested by Working,[9] markets are by nature never black or white; rather there is empirical evidence for price stabilizing as well as price destabilizing effects. The latter can be caused by illiquid markets, herding behaviour, and other types of positive-feedback trading that may add noise to the market and impair price discovery.[10] Although these effects appear less frequently and are relatively weak,[11] they are a reason many investors decide to exclude agricultural derivatives from their portfolios or commodity derivatives overall. However good the intentions, such behaviour may have adverse market effects.

Excluding commodity derivatives (most frequently applied to agricultural derivatives) contributes on average to higher price volatility.[12] Nonetheless, derivative investments which do not consider possible short-term price distorting effects may temporarily impair price discovery. Thus, a sustainable investor in derivatives markets should consider the dynamic behaviour of markets and apply an active investment approach that excludes futures contracts where financial investments have measurable destabilizing price effects. Such active and more selective investment approaches are still rare, but a few providers (academic institutions) already offer signals to filter out potential price distorting effects.[13]

Physical Commodity Investments

Physical commodity investors trade for immediate delivery. With the exception of precious metals, such as gold or silver, physical investments play a minor role in the commodity markets as investors usually avoid the expensive handling of physical commodities.

In contrast to derivative investments, physical investments create additional physical demand and directly influence spot markets. Their transactions have an impact on the production, refining, processing, transportation, and storage of the specific commodity. Thus, ESG issues of physical commodity investments are related to (1) price impact, as well as (2) social and environmental issues along the value chain (traceability).

— (1) Price impact: A physical investor is a "speculative" storage holder competing with other storekeepers as well as consumers for available supply.[14] They maximise expected profits by buying when prices are low and selling when prices are high.[15] Thereby, they help to absorb oversupplied markets and, in case of shortages, they provide additional supply by selling their holdings. Hence, their investment strategies smooth intertemporal price fluctuations but cause harm as soon as they corner the market by acquiring a dominant position in an asset in order to manipulate its price,[16,17] try to create a physical shortage (intentionally), or begin with careless hoarding.[18]

— (2) Traceability: Storage holders are part of the value chain, which stands in relation to social and environmental issues. Traceability helps gain increased transparency on the standards applied in the different parts of the value chain and improves them by applying advanced and independently audited ESG standards.[19]

Conclusion

Derivatives investors should aim to minimise price distortion effects in futures markets. Excluding commodity derivatives is not recommended due to the fact that lower liquidity generally limits commercial hedgers' ability to insure price risks, which is a vital element in global food security. An investor making physical investments directly impacts spot prices and the real economy. Accordingly, physical investors should neither engage in market cornering nor contribute to the market by hoarding, which might lead to a (intentional) shortage. Furthermore, the physical investors should consider, whenever possible, a traceable underlying for investments. Sustainable physical commodity investment standards are still underdeveloped. Investors should consequently engage in further developments of these approaches.

Endnotes

[1]Investments in companies from the mining, oil, and gas or commodity-linked sectors fall in the category of debt and equity investing and are thus covered by other chapters of this Handbook.

[2]List is not exhaustive.

[3]Financial investors close out futures contracts before expiry in order to avoid physical delivery.

[4]See Bellemare, M. F., Barrett, C. B., & Just, D. R. (2013). The welfare impacts of commodity price volatility: Evidence from rural Ethiopia. *American Journal of Agricultural Economics, 95*(4), 877–899; Clapp, J. (2009). Food price volatility and vulnerability in the global south: Considering the global economic context. *Third World Quarterly, 30*(6), 1183–1196; Gilbert, C. L., & Morgan, C. W. (2010). Food price volatility. *Philosophical Transactions of the Royal Society of London B: Biological Sciences, 365*(1554), 3023–3034.

[5]See United Nations. (2015). Transforming our world: The 2030 agenda for global action (p. 13).

[6]See Keynes, J. (1930). *A Treatise on money,* vol. 2. London: Macmillan; Friedman, M. (1953). *The case for flexible exchange rates,* Essays in Positive Economics. Chicago: University of Chicago Press.

[7]For a comprehensive overview of the literature, see Cheng, I. H., & Xiong, W. (2014). Financialization of commodity markets. *Annual Review of Financial Economics, 6*(1), 419–441; Haase, M., Seiler Zimmermann, Y., & Zimmermann, H. (2016). The impact of speculation on commodity futures markets—A review of the findings of 100 empirical studies. *Journal of Commodity Markets, 3*(1), 1–15.

[8]For example, farmers, producers, processors, or physical trading companies.

[9]See Working, H. (1960). Speculation on hedging markets. *Food Research Institute Studies, 1,* 185–220.

[10]See Shiller, R. J., Fischer, S., & Friedman, B. M. (1984). *Stock prices and social dynamics.* Brookings papers on economic activity, pp. 457–510; Shleifer, A., & Summers, L. H. (1990). The noise trader approach to finance. *Journal of Economic Perspectives, 4*(2), 19–33; Steen, M., & Gjolberg, O. (2013). Are commodity markets characterized by herd behaviour? *Applied Financial Economics, 23*(1), 79–90 or Babalos, V., Stavroyiannis, S., & Gupta, R. (2015). Do commodity investors herd? Evidence from a time-varying stochastic volatility model. *Resources Policy, 46,* 281–287.

[11]See Cheng and Xiong (2014).

[12]See, for example, Irwin, S. H., & Sanders, D. R. (2011). Index funds, financialization, and commodity futures markets. *Applied Economic Perspectives and Policy, 33*(1), 1–31. Or Bohl, M. T., & Stephan, P. M. (2013). Does futures speculation destabilize spot prices? New evidence for commodity markets. *Journal of Agricultural and Applied Economics, 45*(4), 595–616.

[13]For more information, visit http://www.commodityclub.ch/.

[14]See Gustafson, R. L. (1958). Implications of recent research on optimal storage rules. *Journal of Farm Economics 40*(2), 290–300 or Wright, Brian. (2014). Global biofuels: Key to the puzzle of grain market behavior. *Journal of Economic Perspectives, 28*(1), 73–97.

[15]See Deaton, A., & Laroque, G. (1996). Competitive storage and commodity price dynamics. *Journal of Political Economy, 104*(5), 896–923 or Routledge, B. R., Seppi, D. J., & Spatt, C. S. (2000). Equilibrium forward curves for commodities. *Journal of Finance, 55*, 1297–1338 for further reading.

[16]For example, the Hunt brothers and the silver market.

[17]Kyle, A. S., & Viswanathan, S. (2008). How to define illegal price manipulation. *American Economic Review, 98*(2), 274–279.

[18]See Jarrow, R. A. (1992). Market manipulation, bubbles, corners and short squeezes. *Journal of Financial and Quantitative Analysis, 27*(3), 311–336 or Ledgerwood, S. D., & Carpenter, P. R. (2012). A framework for the analysis of market manipulation. *Review of Law & Economics, 8*(1), 253–295.

[19]See Knoepfel, I., & Imbert, D. (2012). *The responsible investor's guide to commodities.* On Values Ltd.

Part 3: Special Themes

19. Climate Change and Associated Risks for Investors

Dr. Maximilian Horster
Managing Director, ISS-Ethix Climate Solutions

Climate change has been propelled to the forefront of many investors' minds. Governments and civil society actors are both interested in and concerned about the environmental consequences of large investors' climate impact, with the "divest from fossil fuels" movement driving climate change up the agenda. Research like Carbon Tracker's "Carbon Asset Risk: From Rhetoric to Action"[1] and the report "Developing 2°C Compatible Investment Criteria"[2] (co-authored by 2 Degree Investment Initiative and German Watch) as well as sell-side research have hugely increased awareness of this topic. The 2015 Paris Climate Conference (COP 21) ended with the world committing to curb global warming at 2°C. This implies a radical transformation of the world's economy and, therefore, investor thinking. Some investments will be at risk, while others will benefit.

Investors face different dimensions and levels of climate change–related risk. Such risks can be roughly divided into asset level risk and direct investor risk.

Asset Level Risk

- Climate change effects on the global economy and physical risk for individual assets:

  This can be, for example, extreme weather events impacting a company's production facility. The insurance industry is dealing with such risks in the context of insuring disasters.[3]

- Carbon pricing risk for underlying assets:

  This might include installations that become subject to carbon pricing, such as national or international taxes or cap & trade systems. The European Union Emissions Trading Scheme (EU ETS), for example, is the largest cap & trade system, covering over 11,000 factories in 31 countries.[4] The profits and losses (and therefore stock and bond prices) of companies will be impacted by such systems once carbon prices increase. Hence, it becomes a concern for investors.

- Regulatory risk for assets of certain sectors or operating in specific geographies:

  Climate change–related regulations could hit investments. Air pollution in China, for example, frequently leads to factory closures or city-wide bans on large vehicles.

- Litigation against high-carbon emitters and investors:

  Natural catastrophes linked to climate change pose a threat to companies with the largest climate impact, as they could be made liable for the damage. Such "carbon litigation" has been attempted in hundreds of cases, such as Typhoon Haiyan and Hurricane Katrina.[5]

Investor-Level Risk

- Stranded assets[6] and "carbon bubble" risk:

  Portfolio holdings can be potentially overvalued due to stranded assets. The world agreed to limit global warming to below 2°C at COP 21. Consequently, companies that either own or are dependent on fossil fuel reserves will be impacted as these reserves can no longer be burned. The respective companies might lose some or all of their value, an effect described as "stranded assets risk."

- Investment risk:

  Research has shown that climate-harming companies have a tendency to financial underperformance. In December 2015, 14 major funds with USD1 trillion under management were found to have missed USD22 billion in returns by investing in companies that harm the climate.[7]

- Regulatory risk for investors posed by financial market regulation related to climate change:

  Regulators can demand climate-compliant investments or close in on profits generated through climate-harming investments. Since 2016, France is asking its investors to explain whether their strategies are in line with French climate targets. California is demanding similar transparency from 1,200 insurance companies. In the UK and other European countries, the debate about climate risks has also started, and the EU is coming forward with a High-Level Expert Group on Sustainable Finance.[8]

- Technology risk/innovation disruption:

  Focus on climate change promotes interest and investment in alternative and less carbon-intense technologies. These can disrupt the business models of climate-harming industries that miss the respective developments.

- Reputational risk for investors associated with "financing climate change":

  Amongst others, the "divestment" campaign[9] is very vocal, calling out those investors that have particularly climate-harming assets in their portfolio.[10]

A First Step for Investors: Investment Carbon Footprinting

Investors approaching climate risk for the first time typically do so by running an "investment carbon footprint." This standardised analysis compares a portfolio's carbon intensity against a benchmark. It serves as a portfolio heat map in almost any asset class, with the aim of understanding the climate-relevant sectors and companies.[11] An investment footprint is only a start and cannot replace a bottom-up risk analysis.[12] The analysis should therefore be complemented with more specific data where it matters for the specific investor: evaluating indirect (Scope 3) emissions and avoided emissions, fossil reserves analysis, utility generation mix, forward-looking indicators on companies' climate strategy, 2 degree scenario compliance checks, etc.

Investment Opportunities

Understanding the climate impact of investments, however, can also yield investment opportunities. These opportunities include:

- Financial outperformance of leaders or disruptors: Research has shown that climate-friendly companies deliver higher returns on investments and more stable dividends and have lower costs of capital.[13]

- Rise of new climate-focused or -friendly asset classes: This is especially true in the area of clean tech investments or green bonds. In general, climate change poses the challenge to rethink asset allocation entirely in order to avoid related risks and seek opportunities.[14]

- Identification of new and/or tilted investment approaches and strategies across all asset classes.[15]

- Contributing to investee climate resilience by means of engagement and shareholder action: Groups, such as the Institutional Investors Group on

Climate Change (IIGCC), and initiatives, such as "Aiming for A" and "Climate Action," collectively engage in the topic of climate change with successes at the annual shareholder meetings of such oil giants as BP, Shell, and Total.[16]

Reactions to Carbon Risk and International Trends

The investment community displays a different set of reactions regarding this paradigm shift of factoring climate change into its investment agendas. In general, the community and its stakeholders can be divided into three groups. To this day, the largest group has not yet tackled the topic, although a certain level of awareness exists. The second largest group aims to understand and create internal and external transparency about climate impact. The third group is already taking action on its climate impact.

By the end of 2016, almost 150 investors—mostly from Europe, the US, and Australia and with over USD10 trillion assets under management—had voluntarily created transparency about their investment carbon footprint under the Montreal Carbon Pledge. Governments are also on the move: At the end of 2015, the French government introduced new legislation making it mandatory for French institutional investors to analyse and disclose the climate impact of their investments, starting in 2017.[17] An increasing number of investors are using transparency labels to communicate their analysis efforts to stakeholders.[18]

By mid-2017, the 29+ members of the Portfolio Decarbonization Coalition, with USD600 billion assets under management, had gone a step further and announced they would reduce the greenhouse gas emissions of their portfolios. It is apparent that impact reduction is the next step after transparency. This creates opportunities for related investment products. The Low Carbon Investment Registry already lists 590 emission-reduction investment strategies by 240 investors and managers.

A true game changer was the constitution of the Task Force on Climate-Related Financial Disclosure (TCFD) in 2016. Originally launched as a self-governing industry initiative by corporates and investors alike under the leadership of the Financial Stability Board, it was acknowledged by the G20 Summit in Hamburg in 2017. Today, it is one of the key drivers for improved and standardised climate risk reporting of companies and investors.[19]

The range of taxonomies for climate impact reductions differs widely. Divesting from fossil fuels, a wide range of low carbon indices,[20] positive climate impact funds, clean tech investments,[21] carbon offsetting, shareholder resolutions, or climate-specific engagement strategies are all parts of the same toolbox for an investor. While reactions to investment climate risk differ significantly between investors, it has become apparent that every investor will have to take a position on this topic in the mid-term.

Switzerland and Climate Risk

In 2015, the Swiss Ministry for the Environment commissioned a study on the risk of a carbon bubble for the Swiss financial marketplace.[22] The study included an analysis of the emission exposure of indices commonly used by Swiss investors. The results for the MSCI World are displayed in **Figure 23**. They show, for example, that utilities with a portfolio weight of only 3% are responsible for over 40% of the financed emissions. Further, the analysis revealed that Swiss investors would lose up to 40% of their investment returns if they were made to pay for the greenhouse gases associated with their investments. The study also concluded that most Swiss professional investors have yet to embrace the topic of climate change. This is quite surprising as Switzerland leads the field with the majority of the world's prominent

Figure 23. MSCI World—Sector Exposures and Related Financed Emissions

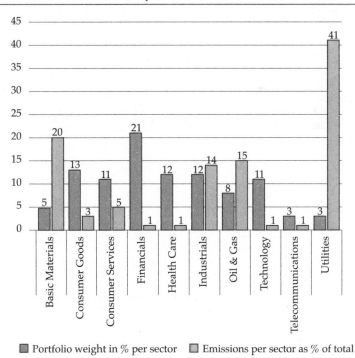

Source: Carbon Risks for the Swiss Financial Centre, BAFU (2015).

and most innovative providers of investment climate impact measurements being based in Switzerland: Carbon Delta, InRate, and ISS-Ethix Climate Solutions.[23] There are signs for transition, however: A 2017 voluntary climate risk analysis for Swiss institutional investors saw a surprisingly high response rate.[24]

Conclusion

Climate impact measurement for investments is becoming a standard in many countries. With stronger government commitment towards a low carbon economy (COP 21) and increasing societal focus on the topic, understanding the impact of climate change regulation is important for institutional asset owners. This includes implementing measurements and strategies to address climate change and related legislation both as a risk and as an opportunity. An established first step for an investor is to undertake a portfolio carbon footprint analysis.

Further Reading

- Decarbonizer. (2016). *Homepage.* Available at: www.decarbonizer.co.

- Global Investor Coalition on Climate Change. (2016). *Low Carbon Investment Registry.* Available at: http://globalinvestorcoalition.org/low-carbon-investment-registry/.

- Montreal Carbon Pledge. (2016). *Homepage.* Available at: www.montrealpledge.org.

- Portfolio Decarbonisation Coalition. (2016). *Homepage.* Available at: http://unepfi.org/pdc/.

- YourSRI. (2016). *Homepage.* Available at: www.yoursri.com.

- 2 Degrees Investing. (2016). *Homepage.* Available at: http://2degrees-investing.org/.

Endnotes

[1]Carbon Tracker Initiative. (2015). *Carbon asset risk: From rhetoric to action.* Available at: http://www.carbontracker.org/report/carbon-asset-risk-from-rhetoric-to-action/.
[2]2 Degrees Investing. (2016). *Studies.* Available at: http://2degrees-investing.org/#!/page_ Resources.
[3]Financial Stability Board. (2015). *Proposal for a disclosure task force on climate related risk.* Available at: http://www.financialstabilityboard.org/2015/11/fsb-proposes-creation-of-disclosure-task-force-on-climate-related-risks-2/.

[4]European Commission. (2016). *The EU Emissions Trading System*. Available at: http://ec.europa.eu/clima/policies/ets/index_en.htm. Over 60 countries and cities already have, or are currently developing, carbon pricing mechanisms. See: http://www.worldbank.org/content/dam/Worldbank/Highlights%20&%20Features/Climate%20Change/carbon-pricing-map-900x476-c.jpg.

[5]Columbia Law School. (2015). *Non-U.S. Climate Change Litigation Chart*. Available at: http://web.law.columbia.edu/sites/default/files/microsites/climate-change/files/_non-u.s._litigation_chart_nov_2015_update.pdf.

[6]EY. (2015). *Let's talk: Sustainability. Special edition on stranded assets*. Available at: http://www.ey.com/AU/en/Services/Specialty-Services/Climate-Change-and-Sustainability-Services/EY-lets-talk-sustainability-issue-4-stranded-assets-from-fact-to-fiction.

[7]Corporate Knights. (2015). *What kind of world do you want to invest in?* Available at: http://www.corporateknights.com/reports/portfolio-decarbonizer/fossil-fuel-investments-cost-major-funds-billions-14476536/350.org/.

[8]See, for example: Chan, S.P. (2015). Mark Carney unveils climate change taskforce. *Telegraph*.
    On the EU's High-Level Expert Group, see https://ec.europa.eu/info/business-economy-euro/banking-and-finance/sustainable-finance_en#high-level-expert-group-on-sustainable-finance.

[9]Fossil-free. (2016). *What is fossil fuel divestment?* Available at: http://gofossilfree.org/what-is-fossil-fuel-divestment/.

[10]See, for example, the campaigners' movie, "Do the math": 350.org (13 August 2015). *Do the math—The movie*. Available at: http://act.350.org/signup/math-movie/?

[11]Institutional Investors Group on Climate Change. (2015). *Investor guide to carbon footprinting*. Available at: http://www.iigcc.org/files/publication-files/Carbon_Compass_final.pdf?iframe=true&width=986&height=616.

[12]2 degrees Initiative. (2015). *Carbon intensity ≠ Carbon risk exposure*. Available at: http://2degrees-investing.org/IMG/pdf/rapport_correlations_en_v8_combined.pdf?iframe=true&width=986&height=616.

[13]CDP. (2015). *Climate action and profitability*. Available at: https://www.cdp.net/CDPResults/CDP-SP500-leaders-report-2014.pdf.

[14]Mercer. (2015). *Investing in a time of climate change*. Available at: https://www.mercer.com/our-thinking/investing-in-a-time-of-climate-change.html.

[15]This includes divestment strategies, low-carbon investment alternatives, decarbonisation strategies, hedging of carbon risk by investing in climate change winners, and carbon-positive investments, including real assets in the forestry space. See: http://www.unepfi.org/fileadmin/documents/climate_strategies_metrics.pdf.

[16]TriplePundit. (2015). *Majority of BP shareholders vote for climate change resolution*. Available at: http://www.triplepundit.com/2015/04/majority-bp-shareholders-vote-climate-change-resolution/.

[17]The Swedish government in 2015 also demanded its governmental pension funds, the AP funds, to disclose their investment footprint.

[18]For example: SEB Group. (2014). *SEB's Ethical Sweden Fund granted climate label*. Available at: http://sebgroup.com/press/news/seb-ethical-fund-sweden-granted-climate-label.

[19]See https://www.fsb-tcfd.org/.

[20]Solactive. (2016). *Solactive launches Low Carbon Index Family—A smart way for investor to take action on climate change.* Available at: http://www.solactive.com/press-releases/solactive-launches-low-carbon-index-family-a-smart-way-for-investor-to-take-action-on-climate-change-2/.

[21]Technologyfund. (2016). *Homepage.* Available at: http://www.technologyfund.ch/.

[22]Bundesamt für Umwelt. (2015). *Kohlenstoffrisiken für den Schweizer Finanzplatz.* Available at: http://www.news.admin.ch/NSBSubscriber/message/attachments/41526.pdf.

[23]ISS-Ethix Climate Solutions is the former financial industry arm of the South Pole Group.

[24]http://www.transitionmonitor.ch/.

Case Study: Nest Collective Foundation

A pioneer in sustainable investment places greater emphasis on the carbon intensity of its portfolios.

Information on the organisation	
Type of organisation	Pension fund
Assets under management (as of 31.12.2016)	CHF2.26 billion
Approximate asset allocation (as of 31.12.2016)	**Asset allocation by asset class:** CHF bonds and loans: 20% Global bonds: 6% Swiss equities: 7% Global equities: 24% Real estate: 25% Others: 18% (Private equity, ILS, credit instruments, infrastructure, liquidity) **Asset allocation by region:** Swiss assets: 54%, before foreign currency hedging Global assets: 41%
Information on the organisation	
Who initiated the drafting of a sustainable investment policy?	In the early 1990s, the Nest Board of Trustees already added social and environmental criteria to the investment guidelines at the request of the Investment Committee. The aim was to ensure that the values of the institution and the pension fund beneficiaries are reflected in the investment policy. The more than 15,000 members of the Nest Collective Foundation also represent the values and objectives of Swiss public policy, which is geared towards the principle of sustainable development.
What was the main motivation for this step?	The discussions, held over 20 years ago, focused on how investments could be made in an environmentally and socially responsible manner. At that time, the spotlight was on other environmental themes, such as air pollution or waste management. Even so, it was already clear back then that preference should be given to green forms of energy, while energy generation with negative environmental externalities should be avoided.

What are the main components/content of the sustainable investment policy?	The investment policy of the Nest Collective Foundation aims to promote sustainable business practices. The sustainability policy is based on two main pillars: the exclusion of negative business activities and the active selection of positive types of business. The first pillar considers guidelines, such as the Global Compact, and is meant to ensure that Nest invests only in economic activities that are compatible with generally recognised standards and conventions and that do not conflict with sustainable business practices. The second pillar involves the preference for financing environmentally and socially efficient economic activities based on an efficiency rating.
	The sustainable investment policy supplements the usual guidelines and objectives regarding risk/reward, governance, and investment process. Under the investment guidelines, as long as alternatives are available within the asset class in question, preference must always be given to the more environmentally efficient investment. The same logic applies to carbon intensity. Therefore, the analysis compares different forms of energy generation across the sectors (e.g., coal-fired power stations versus wind farms) and selects the most eco-efficient method for the sustainable investment universe ("best-in-service" approach).
	Portfolio management takes the Nest sustainability universe as a starting point and then invests according to financial criteria, such as share valuation or bond rating.
How was the sustainable investment policy implemented?	The sustainability policy—and therefore the portfolio's tilt towards low carbon intensity—is anchored in the investment guidelines. Carbon intensity is one element considered in the environmental rating process.
	Nest manages its assets by granting external mandates and has relationships with several asset managers. The actively managed portfolios are measured against common market benchmarks. Nest provides the investable sustainability universe to the asset managers. Separating sustainability research and asset management ensures that all portfolios are managed according to the same criteria. The carbon intensity of the equity portfolios has been recorded since 2015 and compared with a set target value.
What resources have been deployed for this?	Based on the Nest investment guidelines, the sustainability rating company Inrate compiles the sustainable investment universe. An external specialist supports Nest in reporting the impact of sustainability on portfolio construction for listed shares. The other process steps, such as issuing mandates and reporting, are carried out internally.

What were your experiences with policy implementation?	Implementation is essentially quite straightforward because it is based on a clearly defined sustainable investment universe. It does require a little more coordination, as several parties are involved. However, the additional resources still lie within the usual range of costs of active mandates and are mainly required during the implementation of a new portfolio.
	The best-in-service approach, which systematically identifies eco-efficient companies, also automatically leads to a portfolio with a low carbon footprint, as confirmed by values calculated ex-post. This fact remains true, although the portfolio has not been optimised to ensure minimal carbon intensity.
What were notable difficulties?	The biggest challenge is probably to ensure clear communication between all parties involved in order to avoid any misunderstandings. This is particularly important as Nest is breaking new ground with its approach.
What do you consider to be the main benefits of your sustainable investment policy?	With this approach, Nest was able to translate the institution's and members' values in a coherent manner and at the same time implement a successful investment strategy. Given the backdrop of greater awareness of sustainability themes (climate change, human rights), the investment policy also helps to protect the foundation's reputation.

20. The Role of Indices in Sustainable Investment

Kelly Hess
Project Manager, Swiss Sustainable Finance

Konstantin Meier
Manager, PwC

Introduction

Investors' awareness for the importance of corporate sustainability is constantly rising. Therefore, investors are exploring ways to integrate various factors—such as environmental, social, or governance—into their investment strategies. For a sound implementation of such strategies, investors need reliable indices consistent with their approaches and investment scope. Sustainability indices have been available for over 25 years, offered in many different forms depending on investor needs. Such indices, unlike traditional indices, additionally consider sustainability as a factor for inclusion or weighting schemes of companies represented within an index. These indices can incorporate general sustainability criteria (i.e., ESG—environmental, social, governance), thematic considerations (i.e., clean energy, water scarcity), or exclude various controversial sectors (i.e., alcohol, tobacco, nuclear energy, weapons). There are two fundamental roles sustainability indices can play in the context of investments.[1] They can be used in place of traditional indices to manage active strategies based on a sustainable investment universe when managers wish to have a more appropriate starting universe and/or comparison for their own sustainable investment portfolio. They are also used to implement passive strategies (i.e., index tracker funds, ETFs) that reflect sustainability considerations. Through the incorporation of sustainability considerations in the initial index selection, these types of indices in essence are often considered "semi-passive" in that the index itself is based on an active rules-based selection of stocks and bonds, which leads to a tracking error to traditional indices. Such indices have also shown their merit in encouraging companies to continuously develop and improve their sustainability strategies; companies often use their inclusion in such indices as verification of their sustainability commitments vis-à-vis investors. The recently published recommendations of the Task Force on Climate-Related Financial Disclosures,[2] which specifically but not exclusively addresses financial sector organisations, will further lead to companies improving their sustainability strategies. Furthermore, increasing public disclosure leads to greater transparency on ESG risks and opportunities, which is a crucial factor for companies to be included in sustainability indices. There have been promising first signs of large investors starting to adopt sustainable indices, with the announcement in July 2017 by SwissRe that they will be shifting to ESG Benchmarks for their equity and fixed-income portfolios.[3]

The sustainability index landscape. Over the last twenty years, sustainability indices have made their way into the product offering of most index providers (i.e., MSCI, S&P, FTSE, STOXX, Solactive). Originally, only sustainable equity indices were available due mostly to the ease in applying sustainability factors to equities as opposed to fixed income, where other factors such as maturity, currency, and subordination come into play. However, with growing demand from investors, further offerings of sustainable indices and benchmarks are developing. In the last 5 years, the market has expanded and sustainability considerations are used for more and more equity indices and have also been integrated into various fixed-income indices[4] (i.e., S&P ESG Sovereign Bond Index family, Barclays MSCI ESG Fixed-Income Indices), a welcome development for institutional investors who normally invest the majority of their assets in fixed income.

The coverage with regards to region and firm size is growing annually, with most index providers already offering analyses for emerging markets. In addition, although transparency of index rules and the application of sustainability filters have increased dramatically, sustainability indices remain very complex due to the sheer number of sustainability data points (in some cases over 500) applied for the selection of individual titles. This is an issue faced by all index providers and is something investors should carefully consider in order to select an appropriate index that also reflects their own sustainability beliefs. Many index providers have now developed techniques to adjust for undesired factor exposures (i.e., region, size, sector, volatility, leverage) that can occur when selecting sustainable companies from a large mainstream index[5] (i.e., S&P 500, MSCI World). This means that a sustainability index can be constructed to mimic the factor exposure of mainstream indices, hence deviating purely in the so-called "sustainability" or "ESG" factor exposure. This is therefore a very appealing solution for asset owners with strict investment guidelines but who are also targeting higher exposure to sustainable companies or factors.

Currently index offerings are based on various approaches in applying sustainability ratings. Indices can be constructed based on a best-in-class approach (including top-performing companies), on a negative screening/exclusion approach (excluding poor performing companies or specific sectors), or using an alternative weighting scheme (overweighting/underweighting companies based on their sustainability performance). **Table 11** provides an overview of sustainability indices of large providers.

Two Applications of Sustainability Indices in the Investment Process

Index as investment universe and benchmark for active funds. Some investors may choose to implement an active investment strategy with the aid of a sustainability index. They can either choose an existing index or work with a provider on a customised index that best fits their needs. For active strategies, individual titles included in a sustainability index can be used as a starting universe from which the manager selects titles in which to invest. Generally, managers incorporate their own additional selection criteria, which can be purely financial (i.e., profit ratios) but can also include further sustainability criteria (i.e., ESG considerations, thematic/sector exposure) in the selection of their final portfolios. Normally, the chosen index is used both as the starting universe and as the benchmark for performance comparisons. Applying sustainability indices in this way addresses an issue that many portfolio managers face when using traditional indices as performance benchmarks for their investment strategies. Through the use of sustainability indices, sustainable investment strategies are compared to a more appropriate benchmark.

Passive index trackers. Many organisations, especially institutional asset owners, have a large portion of their investments in passive investments. Passive investments, by definition, mimic a defined index and are low-cost solutions to gain exposure to a certain market segment (i.e., region, sector, size). The most common way is to use an existing sustainability index that best fits the desired investment strategy/policy. An alternative is to work with an index provider to customise an index to the specific needs of the investor. It should be noted that an investment based on a sustainability index has elements of active investments as the index is composed based on a sustainability filter and thus usually has a tracking error to a broad market index and can be referred to as "semi-passive." The investor can launch an index tracker fund or use passive mandates that invest in the positions of the chosen sustainability index. This is a relatively cheap and efficient method to implement a sustainability strategy.

Table 11. Overview of Sustainability Indices from Large Index Providers

Sustainability Index	Type	Methods Applied for Component Selection and Weighting	Regional Coverage	Research	Index Provider	Start
Dow Jones Sustainability Indices (DJSI)	Equity	• Best-in-Class • Alternative weighting schemes • Negative screening/exclusions (optional)	Global	RobecoSAM	S&P DJ Indices	1999
S&P ESG Indices	Equity	• Alternative weighting schemes	Global	RobecoSAM	S&P DJ Indices	2016
STOXX ESG & Sustainability Indices	Equity	• Best-in-Class	Global	J. Safra Sarasin/ Sustainalytics	STOXX	2001
MSCI ESG and SRI Indices	Equity	• Best-in-Class • Negative-screening/exclusions (Standard exclusions mandatory)	Global	MSCI ESG	MSCI	2007
FTSE4Good Indices	Equity	• Best-in-Class • Negative-screening/exclusions (Standard exclusions mandatory)	Global	FTSE	FTSE	2001
SXI Switzerland Sustainability 25®	Equity	• Best-in-Class	Switzerland	Sustainalytics	SIX Swiss Exchange	2014
S&P ESG Sovereign Bond Index	Bond	• Alternative weighting schemes	Europe	RobecoSAM	S&P DJ Indices	2015
Barclays MSCI ESG Fixed-Income Indices	Bond	• Best-in-Class • Alternative weighting schemes • Negative-screening/exclusions (optional)	Global	Barclays and MSCI ESG	MSCI	2013

(continued)

Table 11. Overview of Sustainability Indices from Large Index Providers (continued)

Sustainability Theme	Selected Thematic Equity Indices
Low Carbon	• MSCI Low Carbon Indexes • S&P Fossil Fuel Free Index Family • STOXX Low Carbon Index Family • Solactive SPG Low Carbon
Alternative Energy	• S&P Global Alternative Energy Index • World Alternative Energy Index (Société Générale and RobecoSAM) • Solactive Alternative Energy Index
Water	• World Water Index (Société Générale and RobecoSAM) • S&P Water Efficient • MSCI Global Sustainable Water Index
Sustainable Development Goals (SDGs)	• MSCI ACWI Sustainable Impact Index • Solactive Sustainable Development Goals World Index

Source: Swiss Sustainable Finance (2016).

Criteria for choosing an index for an investment strategy: Active vs. passive. When choosing an index to use within a passive or active strategy, the consideration of certain criteria in the selection of an index is important. Each investor must align her index choice with her specific needs.

Index characteristics that should be considered include:

a. Asset allocation (asset class, region, sector, size)

b. Evaluation of the sustainability measurement and component selection approach (i.e., best-in-class, exclusions, degree of selectivity)

c. Financial profile in terms of turnover, tracking error, performance, and specific risk figures (i.e., drawdown)

d. Suitability of index for use with further quant tools (i.e., optimisation through value or size tilts)

Only indices that fit an investor's own investment strategy should be considered.

Conclusions

In particular for institutional investors who often have a large portion in passive investments and are under pressure to keep their costs low across all strategies, sustainability indices can be part of an attractive solution. When choosing a sustainability index, it is important for investors to consider:

• The suitability of an index based on its congruence with their own investment strategy

• The use of an "off the shelf" index vs. a customised index incorporating individual investor requirements

• The use of the index as an investment universe and benchmark or as a basis for a passive index tracking investment solution

These ready-made solutions offer an opportunity to implement sustainability strategies in a quick and cost-efficient manner, especially for organisations that do not have their own internal sustainability analysis capacities. Over the years, sustainable index providers have increased their coverage and techniques and can provide innovative and individualised solutions for almost all investment needs.

Further Reading

- Faust, M., & Scholz, S. (Eds.). (2014). *Nachhaltige Geldanlagen: Produkte, Strategien und Beratungskonzepte*. Frankfurt: Frankfurt School Verlag.

Endnotes

[1]Giese, G. (2014). *Sustainability Indizes. In Nachhaltige Geldanlagen*. Frankfurt: Frankfurt School Verlag.

[2]TCDF. (2017). *Recommendations of the Task Force on Climate-Related Financial Disclosures*. Available at: https://www.fsb-tcfd.org/.

[3]SwissRe. (2017). *Swiss Re among first in the re/insurance industry to integrate ESG benchmarks into its investment decisions*. Available at: http://www.swissre.com/media/news_releases/nr20170706_MSCI_ESG_investing.html.

[4]Bloomberg. (2013). *Barclays, MSCI Issue Fixed-Income Sustainability Indices*. Available at: https://www.bloomberg.com/news/2013-06-12/barclays-msci-issue-fixed-income-sustainability-indices.html.

[5]Staub-Bisang, M. (2012). *Sustainable investing for institutional investors*. Hoboken, NJ: Wiley.

Case Study: Swissport Company Pension Fund

A tailor-made passive investment product is developed for a company pension fund.

Information on the organisation	
Type of organisation	Pension fund
Assets under management (as of 31.07.2017)	CHF849 million
Approximate asset allocation (as of 31.07.2017)	**Asset allocation by asset class:** CHF bonds: 13% Foreign currency bonds: 13% Swiss equities: 10% Global equities: 26% Real estate (incl. mortgages): 34% Liquidity: 4% **Asset allocation by region:** Switzerland: 60% Global: 40%
Information on sustainable investment policy	
Who initiated the drafting of a sustainable investment policy?	The initiative to integrate sustainability into the investment policy came from an individual member of the Board of Trustees in 2008. The Board then discussed the topic and in 2009 decided to use sustainable investments for the first time as an initial trial.
What was the main motivation for this step?	When PVS (Personalvorsorge Swissport) was founded, its mission statement already stipulated that all activities must be financed in an ethically responsible manner. The Board of Trustees thought that getting to grips with sustainability was "the right thing to do," as it was very much in the public eye at the time and pressure was mounting from individual employee representatives. Given the fact that the performance of sustainable investments was at least not lower than that of other comparable conventional products and that they offer a way of diversifying risk, the idea was simply to give it a try.

What are the main components/content of the sustainable investment policy?	As a result of the discussion in the Board of Trustees, a passage was added to the mission statement declaring that PVS manage its assets prudently and consider sustainable investments wherever possible. At the same time, a decision was taken to invest 5% of the pension fund's assets in sustainable funds as a first step. The Board then went on to define what "sustainable" means for PVS. The basic principle adopted was the three-pillar model of sustainability that promotes economic, environmental, and social aspects. A number of exclusion criteria were also defined for sustainable investments, including: armaments, alcohol, tobacco, pornography, genetic engineering, child labour, and gambling.
How was the sustainable investment policy implemented?	In 2009, an invitation to tender was issued for sustainable equity funds with the aim of selecting three products based on different approaches. In 2012, a passive sustainable equity fund was developed in collaboration with Zürcher Kantonalbank (ZKB), which meets PVS' criteria and at the same time has a minimal deviation from the MSCI World Index (ex Switzerland).
What resources have been deployed for this?	An external investment consultant was utilised to both support the Board discussion on defining the sustainable investment criteria and to oversee the initial invitation to tender for a suitable product. PVS worked with ZKB to launch a sustainable equity fund that meets the relevant sustainability criteria.
What were your experiences with the policy implementation?	There were very lengthy discussions among Board members before finalising the definition of the Foundation's own sustainability policy. A certain "maturation process" was necessary to finalise the requirements. After the initial experiences, the Board of Trustees was willing to invest in sustainable investments according to the PVS criteria. Yet, since there was no adequately priced investment product with low deviation from the reference index that satisfied the internal criteria, PVS worked with an investment fund provider to develop a suitable product. This step required the active involvement of those responsible for investment decisions on the Board and in the management.
What were notable difficulties?	The most difficult task was forming a consensus among Board members for the definition of a proprietary sustainability policy. PVS concentrated not only on norms-based exclusion criteria but also defined values-based criteria. This required extensive discussion.
What do you consider to be the main benefits of your sustainable investment policy?	The chosen approach made it possible to gradually build up know-how in sustainable investments. Today, about 11% of the total portfolio and around 32% of equity investments are classified as sustainable. The implementation (especially using passive funds) was completed at low cost and has also turned out well in terms of performance. Sustainable investments are in line with PVS' basic principle of ensuring its beneficiaries' payouts are generated in an ethically responsible manner.

21. Transparency of Sustainable Investments

Erol Bilecen
CSR-Management, Raiffeisen Switzerland

Credibility is a crucial requirement for institutional investors. In the case of a pension fund, for example, every member ultimately wants to ensure that his or her pension assets are managed responsibly. Here, transparency helps to create credibility and thereby builds trust.

As far as purely financial aspects are concerned, credibility is already supported by regulation and auditing. When it comes to sustainability factors, however, the field is still wide open—even though there are initial European developments towards formalising these aspects, such as in France and the Netherlands as detailed next (see also chapter 5 on regulatory issues). The most effective way to promote transparency in relation to responsible investment is to document concrete actions that follow stated intentions.

Publication of the Sustainable Investment Policy

For institutional investors, it therefore makes sense to consider precisely how to guarantee transparency even in the initial stages of drafting a sustainable investment policy. The first and easiest step is to publish this investment policy—for example, on the website, in the annual report, or in an image or information brochure. As with every form of communication, the choice obviously depends on the target audience. In the case of a pension fund, the primary addressees are the fund beneficiaries, whereas in the case of a foundation the audience is mainly the public as well as existing and potential donors. Apart from being informed about the actual existence of such a policy, target groups may also be particularly interested in the reasons for its adoption. In the two examples provided above, this may be for financial reasons (e.g., risk mitigation) or ethical motivations, such as a foundation wanting to avoid a controversial investment clashing with its original purpose.

Transparency of the Portfolio Sustainability

Having defined the objective of the sustainable investment policy, more information on its actual implementation is naturally required. In this context, it is important that the information goes beyond the purely financial dimension ("Our sustainable investments have grown in value by x percent") and extends to the attainment of sustainability goals. This can be done on both a qualitative and quantitative level. One way of illustrating sustainability, for example, is to calculate a portfolio's average sustainability rating in the form of a (capital-)weighted arithmetical mean of the sustainability ratings for the individual positions. This value can then be compared with the average sustainability rating of a conventional benchmark and commented upon. Because the format of these ratings is usually an ordinal figure, they provide a comparison of better or worse performance but do not allow for any quantitative statement on the scale of the difference (e.g., "The portfolio is y percent more sustainable than the benchmark.").

In France, asset owners, fund managers, and insurance companies have been legally obliged since 2015 to report the extent to which they take ESG criteria into consideration in their investment processes, which greenhouse gas emissions are linked to the investments, and the ways in which they are helping to support the transition towards a "low carbon" economy. This reflects the growing trend for an increasing number of investors to determine the carbon footprint of their portfolios. They do so by specifying how many tonnes of carbon dioxide are linked to a specific investment sum. The idea behind this trend is simple: As regulatory and market-specific trends progressively oblige companies to reduce the relevant emissions, carbon-intensive investments should become more and more risky. In contrast to the average sustainability rating, an indication of the portfolio's carbon intensity—especially compared with a benchmark—makes it possible to identify the portfolio's quantitative "added ecological value" through a single figure: "Compared to the benchmark, this portfolio was associated with x percent less CO_2 emissions per CHF1,000." This benefit is offset by a few serious drawbacks, however. The figures supplied by the providers in question are mainly based on estimates and moreover only refer to historical data—which is also the case for financial accounting data. Yet, the biggest drawback is that the obtained value only relates to one dimension: climate. Other environmental indicators, along with all the social sustainability criteria, are completely ignored. Finally, yet importantly, it is impossible to accurately determine whether a change in the carbon footprint is actually the result of an environmental or a financial decision.

One approach to resolve the last issue involves mixed sustainability indicators. Zürcher Kantonalbank (ZKB), for example, uses three separate indicators for investment funds covering environmental (CO_2 emissions per sale), social (reputation risk indicator), and corporate governance (a rating) factors. Here the advantage of ESG's three dimensions is met with the difficulty of having to weight one dimension against the other two: When comparing two companies, how much lower should CO_2 emissions be to off-set a certain difference in reputation, for example?

Reporting on the Exercising of Voting Rights

Another area for reporting on the implementation of a sustainable investment policy is the entire topic of exercising of voting rights and, where appropriate, shareholder engagement. As far back as 2002, Swiss law has required pension funds to draft rules on the exercising of their shareholder rights. The Minder Initiative provided fresh impetus to this process, although not particularly popular as its implementation required a fair amount of extra work. For example, pension funds are now obligated to report how voting rights were concretely exercised in the area of compensation. A few investors, especially those from Nordic and Anglo-Saxon countries, go much further than that. They publish statistics on all votes cast and provide further information on the number of companies with whom they have had active dialogue outside the annual general meeting season and which issues were discussed.

These "Voting & Engagement Reports" are important building blocks for reinforcing the credibility of the corresponding sustainability policy. Regarding these reports, there are several points to consider. For example, the success of an engagement can depend on a certain degree of confidentiality. The report must adopt a carefully judged measure of transparency so as not to jeopardise the discussions that are ongoing in the background. When exercising voting rights, it is important that the underlying voting policy is also reflected in the published voting statistics. Especially because a voting & engagement policy is frequently used in relation to non-sustainable portfolio companies, both the successes and the failures (and their consequences) should be clearly addressed. Although this may well lead to discussions with other stakeholders, it is still the best way to foster credibility in the medium to long term.

Transparency Builds Trust

The following case study shows how transparency can help restore previously shaken trust. In December 2007, an investigative TV programme reported that Dutch pension funds held investments in some companies involved in cluster munition manufacturing. As virtually everyone in the Netherlands—as in Switzerland—is a pension fund beneficiary, there was an enormous public outcry; pressure mounted on the providers to act. Pension funds answered this criticism by committing themselves to sell all shares or bonds issued by the companies in question. Shortly thereafter, to prevent similar cases from arising in the future, many pension funds improved their transparency by publishing their entire investment portfolio online for access by their beneficiaries.

Conclusion

Irrespective of the sustainable investment policy an institutional investor chooses to follow, it is generally recommended to communicate the respective initiatives, successes, and even failures to stakeholders in a transparent manner. This is the only way to complete the feedback loop and ensure the continuous improvement and legitimisation of the investment policy. Creating transparency requires a considerable amount of effort, but this effort should then be rewarded with credibility, legitimation, and reduced reputational risks.

Further Reading

- Nest Sammelstiftung. (2017). *Treibhausgas Analyse Aktienportfolio Nest*. Available at: https://www.nest-info.ch/anlagen/nachhaltigkeit/klima-und-co2-report/.

- Norges Bank Investment Management. (2016). *Responsible investment report*. Available at: https://www.nbim.no/en/transparency/reports/2016/responsible-investment-2016/.

- Österreichische Vorsorgekasse. (2016). *Umwelterklärung*. Available at: http://www.vorsorgekasse.at/umwelterklaerung.

- PGGM. (2016). *Annual Responsible Investment Report*. Available at: https://www.pggm.nl/english/what-we-do/Documents/PGGM-Annual-Responsible-Investment-report_2016.pdf.

- PRI. (2016). *Reporting and assessment*. Available at: https://www.unpri.org/about/pri-teams/reporting-and-assessment.

Part 4: Steps to Implementation

22. Implementing a Sustainable Investment Policy—A Practical Guide

Sabine Döbeli
CEO, Swiss Sustainable Finance

This Handbook clearly demonstrates that there are many different forms and methods for integrating sustainability criteria into investment decisions. There are no right or wrong solutions: The various approaches ultimately have different objectives and hence different impacts. When it comes to implementing a sustainable investment policy, there is similarly no standard solution that is equally suitable for all organisations. This chapter describes the key steps that are relevant for defining and implementing a sustainable investment policy (see **Figure 24**). The various measures are all based on common practice as currently observed in Switzerland and elsewhere. They serve as an orientation for members of supervisory bodies as well as for the investment specialists who implement the recommendations.

It should be noted that not all the steps described need to be implemented, and the implementation does not have to occur in the same sequence. Different steps may be relevant depending on the organisation's current position vis-à-vis sustainable investments. It may also be the case that only individual activities are selected during the initial phase and more-systematic implementation ensues at a later point in time. This guide should therefore be seen as a recipe book from which desired items can be chosen to create a fitting meal.

General Information on Sustainable Investments

Putting a sustainable investment policy in place requires a comprehensive discussion at the top management level (board of trustees or directors) to clarify the organisation's motives and objectives. To initiate this discussion, the first step should be to provide information about the overall theme of sustainable investment. The following points can be addressed by way of general introduction:

- Overview of different forms of sustainable investment

- Current national and international trends in sustainable investing

- Activities of peer organisations

- Information on the performance of sustainable investments

Figure 24.   Steps for Implementing a Sustainable Investment Policy

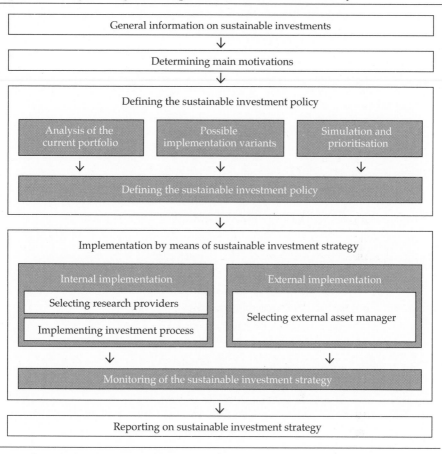

General information on sustainable investments

↓

Determining main motivations

↓

Defining the sustainable investment policy

| Analysis of the current portfolio | Possible implementation variants | Simulation and prioritisation |

↓ ↓ ↓

Defining the sustainable investment policy

↓

Implementation by means of sustainable investment strategy

Internal implementation

Selecting research providers

Implementing investment process

External implementation

Selecting external asset manager

↓ ↓

Monitoring of the sustainable investment strategy

↓

Reporting on sustainable investment strategy

Source: Swiss Sustainable Finance (2016).

This information can be prepared by internal investment specialists, or external consultants can be commissioned to supply it.[1] The provision of essential information on the topic provides the basis for a more in-depth discussion at the top level about the organisation's motivations and objectives.

Determining Main Motivations

The second step involves a discussion at the top management level about the organisation's motivations for becoming involved in sustainable investment.

Input factors for discussing motivations. Senior management or internal investment specialists should prepare various documents as a basis for discussing the organisation's motivations. The following information provides crucial input for this discussion (see also **Figure 25**):

- Organisation's investment policy

- Organisation's statutes

- Initial analysis of the existing portfolio (asset classes, preliminary sustainability review)

- Opinions of internal stakeholders (e.g., supervisory board, employees)

- Opinions of external stakeholders (e.g., beneficiaries, customers, other external stakeholders—for example, in response to surveys or through inclusion of such representatives in discussions)

- Information on regulatory developments

- Societal norms

Figure 25. Input Factors for Determining the Main Motivations

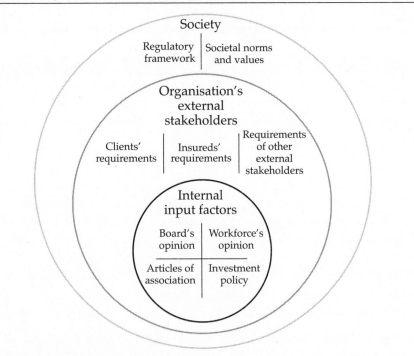

Source: Swiss Sustainable Finance (2016).

Based on this input, the organisation's leadership should establish the objectives of adopting a sustainable investment policy as well as the key motivations.

There are three main motivations, which are not mutually exclusive:

- Compliance with generally recognised national and international norms and/or specific values upheld by the individual organisation

- Improving the risk/return profile of investments

- Promoting sustainable development and sustainable business practices

Compliance with national and international norms and/or the organisation's specific values. The idea behind the first motivation is to reflect certain values in the investment portfolio—irrespective of the financial impact and without seeking to actively influence business practices. This can sometimes be required to abide by certain conventions or can also be done on a voluntary basis.

In Switzerland, it has recently become more important to orient investments towards generally recognised standards, such as international conventions, the Global Compact, or the OECD guidelines for multinational enterprises. This is more than just a coincidence: a recent analysis came to the conclusion that such international guidelines are relevant for investors as well. As a result, even minority shareholders need to review their investments to ensure they do not violate the relevant norms.[2] For example, driven by Publica, large institutional investors have formed their own association, which is committed to the respective goal (see PUBLICA case study after chapter 11). For some time now, the Swiss National Bank has also monitored its investments to make sure they do not conflict with environmental and human rights norms.

Another very common practice is to exclude certain areas that are incompatible with the organisation's values. For example, the personal values of a particular family office led it to exclude gambling, tobacco, armaments, and nuclear energy from its portfolio and concentrate its investments on exceptionally sustainable companies using the best-in-class approach (see Eltaver case study after chapter 8). Or a church organisation might decide to avoid investments in weapons, gambling, and pornography as well as excluding companies with a record of significant human rights abuse.[3]

Although there is a difference between these two approaches—the first is increasingly becoming the standard and is already legally binding in some countries, while the latter is purely a voluntary measure—they have many similarities when it comes to implementation. They are, therefore, dealt with collectively in what follows.

Improving the risk/return profile of the overall portfolio. The second motivation is based on the assumption that it makes financial sense in the short, medium, or long term to take sustainability aspects into consideration when making investment decisions. Here, too, a number of different models are possible. For example, there may be a broad integration of sustainability criteria in the financial analysis stage as this can generate added value in the investment process (see chapters 9.1 and 9.3). Alternatively, individual thematic satellites can be added to the mix in order to improve the risk/return profile of the portfolio as a whole thanks to low correlations (see chapters 12 and 13).

This motivation is closely related to the fiduciary duty of investors managing other people's money to ensure their interests are fully protected. This duty includes the prudent and farsighted management of assets, which experts believe also extends to the integration of ESG factors.[4]

Promoting sustainable business practices. The third motivation can also have different facets. The attempt to actively influence companies to improve their corporate governance and to adopt more responsible and sustainable business practices rests on the premise that these actions ultimately create much better investment opportunities in the long run. Many large international investors (such as California's state pension fund CalPERS or the British BT Pension Fund) and increasingly Swiss investors as well (such as the City of Zurich Pension Fund; see the case study after chapter 9.3) choose this path because they are convinced that promoting prudent and sustainable business practices makes economic sense in the long term. Other organisations consider it important due to ethical considerations to ensure their investments make a positive contribution to sustainable development. In a WWF survey of Swiss pension funds, a contribution towards more sustainable businesses and economic systems is seen as the second biggest motivation for sustainable investments, after fiduciary duty.[5]

In practice, the motivations of organisations involved in sustainable investment often tend to develop in stages. In many cases, there is initially the desire to replicate specific norms and values. At a later stage, ESG factors are integrated into the investment process so as to reduce risks or take advantage of new investment opportunities. In the third phase, the goal is frequently to deploy investments in a way that makes the economy as a whole more sustainable (see **Figure 26**). Here the sequence is not fixed but can follow a different order.

Figure 26.   Evolutionary Development of Motivations for Sustainable Investing

Source: Swiss Sustainable Finance (2016).

As some of the case studies in this Handbook show, the discussion of the main motivations can frequently last over several meetings as there often tend to be different views within boards of trustees/directors so it may take time to reach consensus. In the end, it is important to have a thorough discussion and determine the primary motivation. At the same time, one should not get buried in the discussion of principles. It also should be kept in mind that drafting a sustainable investment policy is ultimately an ongoing process, and other motivations may win importance over time relative to the original motivation.

Defining the Sustainable Investment Policy

Once the main motivation for a sustainable investment policy has been clarified, the practical details can be worked out. This is usually an iterative process where the governing body initially sets the strategic direction by defining the overall conditions (e.g., implementation via existing collective investments, application to only equity and bond positions, gradual and modular implementation). The management then determines which options are available for implementation and what impacts they have (on the investment universe, costs, etc.).

Analysis of the existing portfolio. An important step in this phase is the analysis of the existing portfolio. The following information is key for this step:

- Which asset classes and regions are included in the current portfolio?

- How sustainable is the portfolio already? To this end, all holdings in the portfolio can be analysed based on their sustainability ratings. This analysis highlights which securities have a good, average, or poor sustainability rating. The analysis can also check the extent to which an existing portfolio would be affected by different exclusion criteria.

- Does the portfolio already contain sustainable investments?

- Does the portfolio include asset classes that make it difficult to implement a sustainable investment strategy (e.g., commodities, hedge funds)?

Producing implementation options. Table 2 in chapter 6 provides a comprehensive overview of which approaches—all of which are described in the current Handbook—can practically be applied to which asset classes. **Table 12** builds on this and highlights different implementation options, depending on the existing portfolio components and the defined main motivations, and ranks them according to their suitability.

Diverse implementation options are, of course, available that can be applied to different parts of the portfolio, where it is also possible to combine different approaches. As the examples illustrate, careful analysis of the existing portfolio and the main motivations makes it possible to develop practical options.

Examples for creating sensible options. The portfolio analysis shows which implementation opportunities are available, as the following two fictitious examples illustrate:

- A large proportion of a foundation's portfolio is invested in active equity mandates, and 10% of the relevant portfolio companies have a poor sustainability rating. At the same time, 3% of the companies violate the exclusion criteria that the foundation's board of trustees has deemed important. The primary motivation defined by the board is the wish to bring the investments in line with the foundation's values and goals. When issuing new equity mandates, it may therefore be in the interest of the foundation to take into consideration the relevant exclusion criteria and select companies on the basis of the best-in-class approach in order to avoid companies with poor sustainability ratings.

- The portfolio of a pension fund mainly comprises passively managed bonds and equities denominated in Swiss francs (CHF). The sustainability analysis shows that around 20% of the portfolio has a poor sustainability rating. The main goal set by the board of trustees is to promote sustainable business principles in the long run in order to ensure attractive investment opportunities. At the same time, the board has also specified that investments should continue to be mainly passive in the future. One possible sustainable investment policy could consist of actively exercising the voting rights (globally) for all securities and conducting an active dialogue with companies that have a particularly poor sustainability rating while not modifying the investments themselves.

Option simulation and prioritisation. For each of the options, the impacts on the existing portfolio should be simulated to create a better decision-making basis for selecting the suitable approach. This test can include, for example, whether choosing specific exclusion criteria significantly affects the existing portfolio or whether adopting a best-in-class approach would lead to a major restructuring of the portfolio.

The options can be prioritised based on the following criteria:

- Importance of the asset class within the portfolio

- Impact on the existing investment policy (how much does it need to be changed?)

- Suitability for combination with the existing benchmark

- Impact on the portfolio's risk/return profile

- Availability of respective products and services (feasibility)

- Maximum need for action (biggest impact based on the specified target) as identified by analysis

- Approximate costs

Specifying the sustainable investment policy. After the development of potential implementation options, including a check on their impact on the portfolio and their prioritisation based on criteria relevant to the organisation, the next step is to specify the sustainable investment policy. This defines the underlying goal, which approach is applied to which asset class, and who is responsible for the different elements.

Implementation through a Sustainable Investment Strategy

Figure 27 provides an overview of the elements of a standard investment process in which sustainability factors play a role. In the sustainable investment strategy, the details of the sustainable investment policy are finalised and its implementation planned. The sustainable investment strategy defines how the selected approach is implemented in the various asset classes and includes the following elements:

- List of the ESG factors to be considered

- Strategies and mechanisms used for implementing the policy (e.g., implementation through internal capacities combined with the purchase of

Table 12. Suitability of Different Approaches for Different Asset Classes, Depending on the Primary Motivation

MOTIVATION	RELEVANCE/ SUITABILITY	ASSET CLASS		
		EQUITIES ACTIVE	EQUITIES PASSIVE	CORPORATE BONDS ACTIVE
COMPLYING WITH GENERALLY RECOGNISED STANDARDS AND/OR SPECIFIC VALUES IMPOSED BY THEIR OWN ORGANISATION	High relevance good suitability	— Exclusion criteria — Best-in-Class	— Exclusion criteria	— Exclusion criteria — Best-in-Class
	Medium relevance moderate suitability	— Active voting/ Shareholder engagement — Sustainable thematic investments	— Best-in-Class — Active voting/ Shareholder engagement — Sustainable thematic investments	— Sustainable thematic investments
	Low relevance moderate suitability	— ESG integration		— ESG integration
IMPROVING THE RISK/RETURN PROFILE	High relevance good suitability	— ESG integration — Active voting/ Shareholder engagement		— ESG integration
	Medium relevance moderate suitability	— Best-in-Class — Sustainable thematic investments	— Best-in-Class — Active voting/ Shareholder engagement — Sustainable thematic investments	— Best-in-Class
	Low relevance moderate suitability	— Exclusion criteria	— Exclusion criteria	— Exclusion criteria — Sustainable thematic investments
PROMOTING SUSTAINABLE DEVELOPMENT	High relevance good suitability	— Best-in-Class — Active voting/ Shareholder engagement — Sustainable thematic investments	— Sustainable thematic investments	— Sustainable thematic investments
	Medium relevance moderate suitability	— Exclusion criteria — ESG integration	— Exclusion criteria — Best-in-Class — Active voting/ Shareholder engagement	— Best-in-Class
	Low relevance moderate suitability			— Exclusion criteria — ESG integration

(continued)

Table 12. Suitability of Different Approaches for Different Asset Classes, Depending on the Primary Motivation (continued)

ASSET CLASS

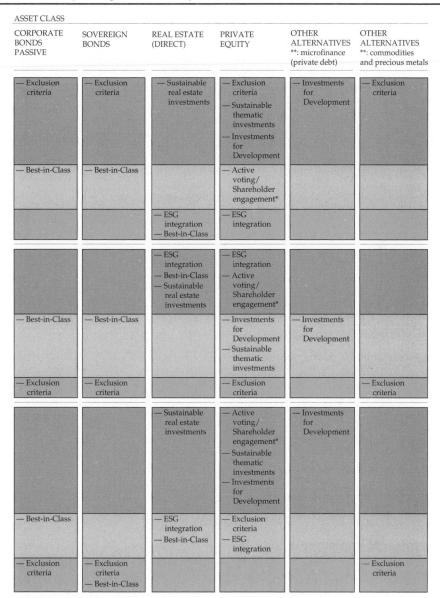

CORPORATE BONDS PASSIVE	SOVEREIGN BONDS	REAL ESTATE (DIRECT)	PRIVATE EQUITY	OTHER ALTERNATIVES **: microfinance (private debt)	OTHER ALTERNATIVES **: commodities and precious metals
— Exclusion criteria	— Exclusion criteria	— Sustainable real estate investments	— Exclusion criteria — Sustainable thematic investments — Investments for Development	— Investments for Development	— Exclusion criteria
— Best-in-Class	— Best-in-Class		— Active voting/ Shareholder engagement*		
		— ESG integration — Best-in-Class	— ESG integration		
		— ESG integration — Best-in-Class — Sustainable real estate investments	— ESG integration — Active voting/ Shareholder engagement*		
— Best-in-Class	— Best-in-Class		— Investments for Development — Sustainable thematic investments	— Investments for Development	
— Exclusion criteria	— Exclusion criteria		— Exclusion criteria		— Exclusion criteria
		— Sustainable real estate investments	— Active voting/ Shareholder engagement* — Sustainable thematic investments — Investments for Development	— Investments for Development	
— Best-in-Class		— ESG integration — Best-in-Class	— Exclusion criteria — ESG integration		
— Exclusion criteria	— Exclusion criteria — Best-in-Class				— Exclusion criteria

*   integral part of private equity investments.
** Only those other alternatives are listed for which sustainable solutions already exist.
Mortgages were not taken into consideration.

Source: Swiss Sustainable Finance (2016).[6]

Figure 27. Integration of Sustainability in Different Elements of the Investment Process (highlighted in yellow)

Management and oversight	Defining responsibility for sustainability policy and strategy
Investment policy	Sustainability themes incorporated into investment policy
Risk management	Sustainability included in the agenda of Investment and/or Risk Committee

Definition of investment strategy / strategic asset allocation	Implementation of investment strategy / tactical asset allocation	Performance monitoring	Reporting
Definition of sustainable investment policy	Implementation of sustainable investment strategy	Regular review of portfolio's sustainability	Reporting on the implementation of the sustainable investment strategy using suitable indicators

Source: Swiss Sustainable Finance (2016).

specific services, or implementation through complete outsourcing as part of the asset management mandate)

- Methods for ensuring and monitoring the implementation process

- Timetable for implementation

- Type of reporting on the sustainable investment strategy (e.g., which key performance indicators [KPIs] are used)

As a rule, two main options can be distinguished for implementing a sustainable investment policy:

- Implementation using the organisation's own asset management resources combined with access to external information

- Complete outsourcing to external asset managers

Internal implementation. If suitable asset management resources are available and sustainable asset management is performed internally, the following steps are relevant.

Selecting research providers. Sustainability information usually is procured from a sustainability research provider as a basis for integrating sustainability factors into asset management.

The selection of the research provider should be done through a comprehensive tender process. The following criteria are important when selecting the provider (not an exhaustive list):

- Research coverage (in terms of asset class, region, and indices)

- Quality/style of research (comprehensive reports, clear summaries, customer ratings, etc.)

- Approach of the research team (compatible with the organisation's own understanding of ESG? Is the research geared more towards ethically or financially relevant criteria?)

- Research capacity (e.g., number of analysts) and update frequency

- Costs (fixed- or volume-based pricing structure, price level)

- Accessibility of research (i.e., via database), support with reporting (i.e., annual reports on engagement)

When deciding on a research provider, one normally commits for a certain period because the incorporation of external research takes time and effort and creates dependencies in the investment process. It is therefore particularly important to invest time in the decision and ensure careful selection.

The choice of a sustainability rating agency is comparable with the selection of an asset manager for a mandate and likewise tends to involve several stages. Based on in-house research, a long list of providers is drawn up and a questionnaire usually sent to them.[7] The submitted documents are assessed based on the defined criteria in order to narrow down the list. The questions that are important to the organisation are then discussed in more detail with the selected providers so as to be able to then choose the most suitable partner.

Implementing the investment process. Once the research provider has been selected, the next step is to define how this research is to be integrated into the investment process. Here the following questions need to be clarified:

- Who is responsible for the sustainable investment process? (See also **Figure 28**.)

- Which criteria must always be integrated in decisions? Which serve only as background information, without necessarily having an influence on the investment decision?

- How is the research made available to the portfolio managers (e.g., integration in an internal asset management system, regular provision

Figure 28. Responsibility for the Different Steps in Defining and Implementing a Sustainable Investment Policy

Steps	Responsible people in the organisation for		
	Insurance companies	Pension funds	Foundations
General information on sustainable investments	Specialist (internal) or external advisor	Specialist (internal) or external advisor	Director or external advisor
Determining main motivations	Management & Board of Directors	Foundation board	Foundation board
Defining the sustainable investment policy			
Analysis, simulation, and implementation variants	Specialists (internal) and portfolio manager	Portfolio managers or external advisor	Director or external advisor
Defining the sustainable investment policy	Management & Board of Directors	Foundation board	Foundation board
Implementation by means of sustainable investment strategy			
Internal implementation or outsourcing to external managers	Specialists (internal) and portfolio manager	Portfolio managers and Investment Committee	Director and Investment Committee
Monitoring	Specialists (internal) and/or portfolio manager	Specialists (internal) and Investment Committee	Director and Investment Committee
Reporting on sustainable investment strategy	Specialists (internal) and/or external asset manager	Specialists (internal) or external asset managers	Director or external asset manager

Source: Swiss Sustainable Finance (2016).

of a sustainable investment universe, access to the research provider's database)?

- How is the sustainable investment process monitored (e.g., flagging sustainable/non-sustainable securities in the asset management system, regular agenda item at investment meetings)?

External implementation. If the second option is chosen and sustainable asset management is completely outsourced, the following steps are relevant.

Selecting external asset managers. By and large, most asset managers now offer sustainable investment management. However, there are significant differences when it comes to their sustainable investment skills. It therefore makes sense to select an external partner based on a comprehensive tender process that carefully reviews the details of their sustainability approach.

In addition to the usual financial criteria, the following aspects need to be reviewed:

- Which approach is the sustainable asset management based on? What are the underlying convictions?

- To which segments (asset classes, product types) does the ESG approach apply?

- Which internal and external resources does the asset manager utilise for sustainability research?

- What experience do the ESG specialists in the asset manager's team have?

- How are the investment specialists' incentive schemes designed? Do they also incorporate ESG factors?

- Is it possible to define customer-specific criteria?

- How is the sustainable investment process structured?

- Is there reporting on the portfolio's sustainability; if so, in which format?

- How is the performance track record for both the sustainable investments and the comparable non-sustainable mandates?

- How high are the costs for sustainable asset management?

Mandates for sustainable asset management are usually tendered when existing mandates expire. To be able to implement a sustainable investment strategy more quickly, dialogue can also be initiated with existing asset managers in order to see whether more sustainability criteria can be gradually introduced into the mandates. For example, an exclusion list of controversial companies could be distributed to all existing portfolio managers, who would then be asked to divest from the relevant securities.

Monitoring the sustainable investment strategy. Irrespective of whether sustainable investments are managed internally or by external asset managers, the implementation of the sustainable investment strategy needs to be regularly monitored.

If the investments are managed internally, one option is to check whether sustainability factors can be made a routine item on the agenda of the investment committee or risk-review meetings. If portfolio managers want to buy a security, they not only have to present the financial arguments for the decision but also the sustainability considerations.

In the case of external asset management, sustainability factors should be part of the periodic performance reviews. An asset manager may also be asked to provide regular reports on sustainability performance. To this end, the average sustainability rating of the portfolio can be calculated or the sustainability ratings of individual positions can be shown in a portfolio overview. This makes it possible to track the sustainability performance of a portfolio and see how it develops over time. Reports on the exercising of voting rights or shareholder engagement activities can also be requested.

Reporting on the Sustainable Investment Strategy

Depending on the type of asset owner, it may make sense to publish a report on the activities in the area of sustainable investment. If the assets are managed internally, such a report can be produced by the portfolio managers or internal sustainability specialists. In the case of external asset management, a clause can be included in the service level agreement to require the asset manager to report regularly on the implementation of the sustainability strategy.

This report might include the following topics:

- Reporting on key indicators, such as the average sustainability rating of the portfolio and its development over time

- Reporting on the exercising of voting rights (percentage of votes for and against on a thematic and geographical level)

- Details on engagement activities (e.g., milestones achieved)

- Case studies on noteworthy sustainable portfolio positions

Table 13.   Examples of Sustainable Investment Reports Provided by Institutional Investors

Institutional Investor	Country	Link to Report	Pages Dealing with Sustainability
Nest Collective Foundation	Switzerland	https://www.nest-info.ch/fileadmin/webdaten/archiv/geschaeftsberichte/Nest_GB15_DE_2015-07-12_def-web.pdf	p. 19
CAP	Switzerland	http://www.cap-prevoyance.ch/la-fondation/documents/rapports	p. 16
PGGM	Netherlands	https://www.pggm.nl/english/what-we-do/Documents/PGGM-Annual-Responsible-Investment-report_2016.pdf	Entire report
AP4	Sweden	http://www.ap4.se/globalassets/formular/rapportarkiv/2016/har-1516/eng/sustainability-and-corporate-governance-report-2015_2016.pdf	Entire report
Norges Investment Bank	Norway	https://www.nbim.no/en/transparency/reports/2016/responsible-investment-2016/	Entire report

Source: Swiss Sustainable Finance (2017).

- Case studies on portfolio positions where the challenges presented have led to the initiation of a dialogue or even divestment

A few examples of advanced reporting on sustainable investment strategies are listed in **Table 13**.

Importance of Embedding Sustainability in the Organisation

Figure 28 illustrates the process described in this chapter and highlights which actors are responsible for the various steps, depending on the type of organisation. It is crucial to consider that the investment policy is approved by the highest supervisory body. This is the only way to ensure that it is also implemented in a consistent fashion.

Responsibility for implementing the policy depends heavily on the institutional investor's organisational structure as well as on the size of the team in question. Therefore, it is virtually impossible to give a universally valid description. Another important consideration is the clear designation of responsibilities for the implementation project.

Conclusions

More and more institutional investors—whether pension funds, insurance companies, or foundations—are starting to integrate sustainability aspects into their investment activity. These organisations differ significantly in terms of size, purpose, structure, and investment portfolio. In this Handbook we attempt to take into consideration the different starting points and situations and differentiate our recommendations accordingly. It is important, however, that the definition of a sustainable investment policy be closely adapted to the specific situation of the individual organisation. This Handbook highlights numerous opportunities for incorporating sustainability into the investment process. It often makes sense to choose a combination of different approaches. In many cases, the sustainability policy is initially integrated into just one or two asset classes before gradually being applied to other asset classes. The process illustrated in Figure 24 is therefore not finished after one iteration. It is rather a continuous cycle in which the investment policy is regularly reviewed and extended or adjusted as necessary.

The market and the environment for sustainable investments are rapidly developing. New products and services are being launched, regulatory changes announced, and new industry standards published at an unprecedented rate. Swiss Sustainable Finance is following these developments very closely and informs members regularly about important trends. A regular dialogue between the different actors—whether between asset owners and providers, associations and the regulator, or stakeholders and institutional investors—ensures the developments are structured to produce maximum benefit for all involved parties. Through its own activities, SSF is also keen to contribute to this dialogue and encourage the development of sustainable investments to the benefit of all.

Further Reading

- Investment Leaders Group. (2016). *Taking the long view, A toolkit for long-term, sustainable investment mandates.* University of Cambridge.

- Kirchenamt der Evangelischen Kirche in Deutschland. (2016). *Leitfaden für ethisch-nachhaltige Geldanlagen in der evangelischen Kirche.*

- PRI. (2012). *Writing a responsible investment policy, guidance for asset owners.*

- PRI. (2016). *How asset owners can drive responsible investment beliefs, strategies and mandates.*

- Staub-Bisang, M. (2012). *Sustainable investing for institutional investors: Risks, regulations and strategies.* Hoboken, NJ: Wiley & Sons.

Endnotes

[1] Information on different forms of sustainable investment, international trends, and activities of other asset owners can be found on the following websites, amongst others: www.unpri. org, www.eurosif.org, www.sustainablefinance.ch.

[2] Jaeggi, O., & Webber Ziero, G. (2016). What new OECD standards mean for investors. *MIT Sloan Management Review—Blog.* Available at: http://sloanreview.mit.edu/article/investors-required-by-oecd-to-broaden-due-diligence/.

[3] Kirchenamt der Evangelischen Kirche in Deutschland. (2016). *Leitfaden für ethisch-nachhaltige Geldanlagen in der evangelischen Kirche* (German only). Available at: http://www.ekd. de/download/ekd_texte_113_2016.pdf.

[4] UN Global Compact, UNEP FI, PRI. (2015). *Fiduciary duty in the 21st century.* Available at: http://www.unepfi.org/fileadmin/documents/fiduciary_duty_21st_century.pdf.

[5] WWF. (2016). *Schweizer Pensionskassen und verantwortungsvolles Investieren* (German). Available at https://assets.wwf.ch/downloads/wwf_shareaction_german_report.pdf.

[6] The weighting of different approaches was carried out by the Editorial Team and is based on the assessment of experts and asset owner representatives.

[7] Some time ago, different research providers were rated on behalf of foundations and their quality compared. SustainAbility assessed sustainability rating agencies as part of the "Rate the Raters" project and in different phases. SustainAbility. (2012). *Rate the raters: Phase five.* Available at: http://sustainability.com/our-work/reports/rate-the-raters-phase-five/.

A few years ago, Novethic also published an overview of different rating agencies. Novethic. (2013). *Overview of ESG rating agencies.* Available at: http://www.novethic.com/fileadmin/user_upload/tx_ausynovethicetudes/pdf_complets/2013_overview_ESG_rating_agencies. pdf.

Appendix

List of Abbreviations

BVV 2	Swiss Federal Law on Occupational Retirement, Survivors' and Disability Pension Plans (BVG)
CHF	Swiss franc
CO_2	Carbon dioxide
DCF	Discounted cash flow
ESG	Environmental, social, governance
FOEN	Federal Office for the Environment
G7	Group of Seven
GM	General meeting
GRESB	Global Real Estate Sustainability Benchmark
IFC	International Finance Corporation
IIGCC	Institutional Investors Group on Climate Change
ILG	Investment Leaders Group
JPY	Japanese yen
KKV	Ordinance on Collective Capital Investments
OECD	Organisation for Economic Cooperation and Development
PRI	Principles for Responsible Investment
ROIC	Return on Invested Capital
SASB	Sustainability Accounting Standards Board
SDGs	Sustainable Development Goals
SMI	Swiss Market Index
SSF	Swiss Sustainable Finance
SVVK-ASIR	Swiss Association for Responsible Investments
UN	United Nations
UN COP 21	UN Climate Conference in Paris 2015

UNGC	United Nations Global Compact
USD	US dollar
VegüV	Ordinance against Excessive Compensation in Listed Corporations
WACC	Weighted average cost of capital
WBCSD	World Business Council for Sustainable Development

Glossary

Carbon bubble. Assumed overvaluations of companies that have fossil fuel assets. In light of the climate protection targets determined in Paris, those fuels may no longer be burned and thus lose their value.

CDP. CDP, originally named Carbon Disclosure Project, is an independent non-profit organisation providing large databases of environmental data on companies. The most well-known database offers insights into carbon emissions and strategies of companies. Apart from carbon data, CDP also provides data on water, forest products, supply chains, and more (www.cdp.net).

CO_2 intensity. CO_2 intensity measures the amount of emitted CO_2 relative to a reference dimension. Within this publication, the concept is used in relation to CO_2 intensity of portfolios, where the comparative dimension is an invested unit (e.g., an investment of CHF1 million).

Corporate governance factors. Governance factors within ESG criteria in the context of investing refer to the system of policies and practices by which a company is governed and controlled. They include but are not limited to transparency on management and Board compensation, independence of Board members, and shareholder rights.

Divestment. Divestment describes the act of selling a security. In this publication, the term is mainly used related to selling of a holding due to a violation of a sustainability criterion defined by an investor.

Environmental factors. Environmental factors within ESG criteria in the context of investing include but are not limited to the environmental footprint of a company or country (i.e., energy consumption, water consumption), environmental governance (i.e., environmental management system based on ISO 14'001), and environmental product stewardship (i.e., cars with low fuel consumption).

ESG. ESG stands for Environmental (i.e., energy consumption, water usage), Social (i.e., talent attraction, supply chain management), and Governance (i.e., remuneration policies, board governance). ESG factors form the basis for sustainability ratings, best-in-class, and integration investment approaches.

ESG criteria. Environmental, social, and governance criteria, forming the foundation of a sustainability analysis.

ESG indices. An ESG or sustainability index is an instrument to measure the value of a selection of the stock market. The index is calculated based on the price of shares that have been selected according to a predetermined sustainable investment approach. Investors use such instruments to trace market development and compare the return of a specific investment product with the overall market return.

ESG performance. Performance of organisations, countries, or issuers with respect to defined environmental, social, or governance criteria.

ESG rating. ESG ratings and sustainability ratings mirror the performance of companies/countries/funds measured against environmental, social, or governance (ESG) factors. Sustainability ratings enable investors to gain a quick overview of the sustainability performance of companies/countries/funds. Such ratings provide the foundation of a best-in-class approach.

ESG reporting. Reporting of an organisation on environmental, social, and governance factors.

ESG shareholder proposals. Shareholder proposals, aiming at the improvement of social, environmental, and governance criteria.

Fiduciary duty. In the institutional investment context, trustees of pension funds owe fiduciary duties to beneficiaries to exercise reasonable care, skill, and caution in pursuing an overall investment strategy suitable to the purpose of the trust and to act prudently and for a proper purpose. The explicit legal nature of fiduciary duty varies depending on the country of origin. While most institutional investment funds strive to create financial benefits for their beneficiaries, it is also possible for trust deeds explicitly to require trustees to consider ESG factors in investments. According to international legal experts, it is part of the fiduciary duty of a trustee to consider such opportunities and risks in investment processes.

Governance factors. See Corporate Governance factors.

Impact investing. Investments made into companies, organisations, projects, and funds with the intention to generate a measurable, beneficial social and environmental impact alongside a financial return.

Materiality. In the sustainability context, information is material if there is a clear link to the financial performance of a company.

Montreal Carbon Pledge. Launched in September 2014, signatories of the Montreal Carbon Pledge commit to measure and publicly disclose the carbon footprint of their investment portfolios on an annual basis (www.montreal-pledge.org).

Portfolio Decarbonisation Coalition. Initiative of institutional investors who have committed themselves with quantitative targets to reduce the CO_2 intensity of their portfolios (http://unepfi.org/pdc/).

Principles for Responsible Investment (PRI). The United Nations–supported Principles for Responsible Investment (PRI) initiative is an international network of investors, asset managers, and service providers working together to put the six Principles for Responsible Investment into practice. Its goal is to understand the implications of sustainability for investors and support signatories to incorporate these issues into their investment decision making and ownership practices (www.unpri.org).

Smart beta. Rules-based methodology for index construction that selects companies based on certain criteria (or factors). It aims to realise risk/return profiles that are superior to the ones of market capitalisation-weighted indices.

Social factors. Social factors within ESG criteria in the context of investing include, but are not limited to, worker rights, safety, diversity, education, labour relations, supply chain standards, community relations, and human rights.

Stranded assets. Stranded assets refer to a scenario in which the value of fossil fuel reserves is reduced due to rising carbon prices or if the extraction of fossil fuels is hindered by regulation and social pressure. The share price of fossil fuel companies could diminish considerably if political pressure to reduce carbon emissions increases. The risks associated with stranded assets is a growing concern for investors.

Sustainable investment. Sustainable investment refers to any investment approach integrating environmental, social, and governance (ESG) factors into the selection and management of investments.

Sustainable development. The Brundtland Commission of the United Nations has defined sustainable development as follows: "Sustainable development is development which meets the needs of current generations without compromising the ability of future generations to meet their own needs."

UNEP FI. UNEP FI is a global partnership between UNEP and the financial sector founded in 1992. UNEP FI's mission is to bring about systemic change in finance to support a sustainable world and is highlighted in its motto, "Changing finance, financing change." Member organisations—representing banking, insurance, and investment—recognize sustainability as part of a collective responsibility and support approaches to anticipate and prevent potential negative impacts of the financial industry on the environment and society (www.unepfi.org).

UNEP Inquiry. UNEP Inquiry into the Design of a Sustainable Financial System is a UNEP programme that works on strategies enabling an alignment of the financial system to the needs of sustainable development, thereby accelerating the transition to a resource-efficient economy.

United Nations Global Compact (UNGC). This UN initiative defined ten principles for responsible practices in business and supports companies in adapting their strategies and activities to comply with these principles. The ten universally accepted principles relate to the topics of human rights, labour, environment, and anti-corruption. Companies signing the UNGC commit to regularly report on progress related to the ten principles (www. unglobalcompact.org).

Imprint

Editors

Swiss Sustainable Finance (SSF) strengthens the position of Switzerland in the global marketplace for sustainable finance by informing, educating, and catalysing growth. The association, founded in 2014, has representation in Zurich, Geneva, and Lugano. Currently SSF unites around 100 institutional members and network partners from financial service providers, investors, universities and business schools, public sector entities, and other interested organisations (www.sustainablefinance.ch).

The preparation of this Handbook was initiated and supported by the "Institutional Asset Owners Workgroup" of Swiss Sustainable Finance, which consisted of the following members: Adnan Ahmad (AXA Winterthur), Claudia Bolli (Swiss Re), Renato Bortolamai (Eltaver AG), Ulla Enne (Nest Collective Foundation), Dr. Hubert Niggli (suva), Pascale Pfeiffer (die Mobiliar), and Kristine Schulze (Helvetia).

CFA Society Switzerland is the non-profit alumni organisation of CFA charterholders and other members of CFA Institute in Switzerland. Founded in 1996, it has more than 3,000 members in all parts of the country. CFA Society Switzerland is the ninth largest of the 149 societies that are affiliated with CFA Institute, the global professional organisation for investment managers with more than 142,000 members.

The mission of CFA Society Switzerland is to promote ethical behaviour and professionalism in the Swiss market and to serve as a catalyst for members to strengthen and expand their professional networks. It conducts regular continuing education workshops in Geneva and Zürich and hosts conferences, such as the Swiss Pensions Conference. CFA Society Switzerland promotes awareness for the CFA charter and brand in the Swiss market and maintains working relations with all relevant stakeholders, such as employers, media, regulators, and other professional organisations. It represents the values of the CFA Institute Code of Ethics and Standards of Professional Conduct to the authorities through its advocacy engagement.

CFA Society Switzerland is a volunteer-driven organisation supported by a staffed office based in Zug, Switzerland. Its website is swiss.cfa, and the CFA Society Switzerland CEO tweets @cfa_ch.

Editorial Team

Ulla Enne, Investment Specialist, Nest Collective Foundation

Pascale Pfeiffer, Corporate Social Responsibility, Head of Sustainability & Art, die Mobiliar

Dominique Habegger, Head of Institutional Asset Management, de Pury Pictet Turrettini & Cie.

Pierin Menzli, Head of Sustainable Investment, J. Safra Sarasin

Sabine Döbeli, CEO, Swiss Sustainable Finance

Jean Laville, Deputy CEO, Swiss Sustainable Finance

Authors

Philip Ammann, CFA, Global Thematic Equities Analyst, Vontobel Asset Management

Roger Baumann, COO & Head Sustainability, Credit Suisse Global Real Estate

Erol Bilecen, CSR-Management, Raiffeisen Switzerland

Dr. Marc-Olivier Buffle, Senior Client Portfolio Manager, Pictet

Bernard de Halleux, Head of Candriam Switzerland LLC, Candriam Investors Group

Angela de Wolff, Founding Partner, Conser Invest

Sabine Döbeli, CEO, Swiss Sustainable Finance

Christian Etzensperger, Head of Corporate Strategy & Chief of Staff, responsAbility Investments AG

Andrea Gäumann, Consultant, BHP—Brugger and Partners Ltd.

Dr. Marco Haase, Head of Research Sustainable Finance, Center for Corporate Responsibility and Sustainability (CCRS), University of Zurich

Adam Heltzer, Responsible Investment, Partners Group

Kelly Hess, Project Manager, Swiss Sustainable Finance

Jonathan Horlacher, CFA, Financial Analyst, Credit Suisse (Switzerland)

Dr. Maximilian Horster, Managing Director, ISS-Ethix Climate Solutions

Vincent Kaufmann, CEO, Ethos Foundation

Antonios Koutsoukis, CFA, Financial Analyst, Credit Suisse (Switzerland)

Jean Laville, Deputy CEO, Swiss Sustainable Finance

Konstantin Meier, Manager, PwC

Philipp Mettler, CFA, Senior Sustainable Investment Analyst, Bank J. Safra Sarasin

Dr. Agnes Neher, Sustainability Manager, Bank J. Safra Sarasin

Basil Oberholzer, Project Manager Financial Services, Global Infrastructure Basel Foundation

Dr. Falko Paetzold, Managing Director, Center for Sustainable Finance and Private Wealth, University of Zurich

Marina Parashkevova, Research Team Leader, Symbiotics SA

Ben Peeters, Senior Investment Specialist SRI, Candriam Investors Group

Catherine Reichlin, Head of Financial Research, Mirabaud & Cie.

Katharina Schneider-Roos, CEO, Global Infrastructure Basel (GIB) Foundation

Peter Sigg, Senior Investment Strategist, LGT Capital Partners

Regula Simsa, CFA, Consultant, BHP—Brugger and Partners Ltd.

Fabio Sofia, Head of Portfolio Advisory, Symbiotics SA

Alex Tobler, CFA, Head of Sustainable Investment, Berner Kantonalbank

Jürg Vontobel, Founder, Vietnam Holding Asset Management

Dr. Daniel Wild, Head of Sustainability Investing Research & Development, Member of the Executive Committee, RobecoSAM AG

Alexander Zanker, CFA, Senior ESG/Quant. Strategist, LGT Capital Partners

Acknowledgements

Swiss Sustainable Finance would like to thank the following people for their valuable contribution to this Handbook:

- Christian Dreyer, CFA, CEO, CFA Society Switzerland, launched the idea of publishing the SSF Handbook in English and gained the support of the CFA Institute Research Foundation and other parties for the project.

- The authors of the different chapters have offered expert knowledge of their respective fields and have constructively incorporated the editorial team's suggestions. Without their know-how, the various topics could not have been covered in such depth.

- Numerous representatives of different Asset Owners have openly shared insights into their sustainable investment strategies, enabling very practical illustrations within the case studies.

- The members of the SSF workgroup "Institutional Asset Owners" launched the idea to prepare this publication and have provided valuable feedback concerning the structure and content of the Handbook during the conceptualisation and implementation phase.

- The editorial team offered their knowledge and time to provide extensive feedback to all the authors on the original texts.

- The SSF team (Sabine Döbeli, Kelly Hess, Jean Laville, Ivo Mugglin, Anna Walker) edited all texts and translations to make them consistent throughout the Handbook and in the different language versions.

- All translators and proofreaders quickly adopted the broad terminology of sustainable investment to create a consistent and comprehensive final text.

Zurich, December 2017

Translations: from French: Dominique Jonkers (Jonkers & Partners, expert financial translators); from German: Graeme High (Graeme High Language Consultants Ltd.).

Applied style of citation in the reference list and further reading section: APA (American Psychological Association).

Disclaimer

This document was prepared by Swiss Sustainable Finance in collaboration with various authors. The information contained in this document (hereinafter "information") is based on sources that are considered as reliable. However, Swiss Sustainable Finance does not assume any liability for their correctness nor completeness. The information can be subject to change at any time without obligation to notify the recipient thereof. Unless stated otherwise, all figures are unaudited and not guaranteed. All actions taken based on the information are at the recipient's own liability and risk. This document is intended for informational purposes only. The information does not release the recipient from exercising his or her own judgement.

RESEARCH FOUNDATION
CONTRIBUTION FORM

☑ **Yes**, I want the Research Foundation to continue to fund innovative research that advances the investment management profession. Please accept my tax-deductible contribution at the following level:

Thought Leadership Circle..................... US$1,000,000 or more
Named Endowment .... US$100,000 to US$999,999
Research Fellow .... US$10,000 to US$99,999
Contributing Donor............................US$1,000 to US$9,999
Friend .... Up to US$999

I would like to donate US$ _____.

☐ My check is enclosed (payable to the CFA Institute Research Foundation).
☐ I would like to donate appreciated securities (send me information).
☐ Please charge my donation to my credit card.
　　　　　　☐ VISA　☐ MC　☐ Amex　☐ Diners

Card Number

____/____

Expiration Date

Name on card　PLEASE PRINT

☐ Corporate Card
☐ Personal Card

Signature

☐ This is a pledge. Please bill me for my donation of US$_____
☐ I would like recognition of my donation to be:
　　☐ Individual donation　☐ Corporate donation　☐ Different individual

PLEASE PRINT NAME OR COMPANY NAME AS YOU WOULD LIKE IT TO APPEAR

PLEASE PRINT　☐ Mr.☐ Mrs.☐ Ms.　MEMBER NUMBER_____

Last Name (Family Name)　　　First (Given Name)　　　Middle Initial

Title

Address

City　　　　　　State/Province　　　Country ZIP/Postal Code

Please mail this completed form with your contribution to:
The CFA Institute Research Foundation • P.O. Box 2082
Charlottesville, VA 22902-2082 USA

For more on the CFA Institute Research Foundation, please visit www.cfainstitute.org/learning/foundation/Pages/index.aspx.